PHILOSOPHY AND THE SOCIAL PROBLEM

The Annotated Edition

WILL DURANT

Winner of the Pulitzer Prize and Medal of Freedom

Edited
by
JAMES BISHOP

To Alden Freeman

Philosophy and the Social Problem

Promethean Press
1846 Rosemeade Pkwy #192
Carrollton, TX 75007
www.promethean-press.com

Manufactured in the United States of America

ISBN 978-0-9737698-6-9

TABLE OF CONTENTS

FOREWORD

In late 1916, in a tiny apartment he shared with his wife in the Bronx area of New York, Colombia University philosophy student Will Durant began work on what would become his first book. "A corner of our bedroom became my study," he would later recall, "a shelf of books by the window provided me with material for reference and pilferage. I used a lamp-clasp from my bicycle to attach a removable drawing board to the right arm of a rocker."[1] Upon this makeshift desk Durant wrote *Philosophy and the Social Problem*, launching a stellar literary career that would span more than six decades and culminate in a Pulitzer Prize and the Presidential Medal of Freedom.

Philosophy and the Social Problem was Will Durant's first attempt at putting his philosophy of Perspectivism into words. The thesis of the book consisted of two parts: first, that philosophy was stuck in a rut, an exercise in ivory tower academics with no application to everyday living and, hence, no audience; and, second, that the social problems plaguing the human race had not found sufficient resolution because previous efforts had failed to unify science and philosophy in pursuit of solutions.

Philosophy and the Social Problem was more than simply Durant's first book; it was his final doctoral thesis at Colombia University. As such, Durant wrote in an academic style more in line with what his professors expected of their students than what Durant's fans would later come to expect of him. It, at times, lacks the colloquial delivery and the melodic prose of Durant's later works. The seeds of Durant's literary evolution are clearly there, however, as Durant used the book to criticize the very academia to whom he submitted his work for their insular, ivory tower academics. Writing the book was no doubt painful to Durant, who addressed an audience that least interested him in a manner in which he disagreed *so that he might express his disagreement*. It would be the first and last time he wrote in such a heavy academic style, as his writing from that point forward focused solely on bringing philosophy and a love of history to the masses, beginning with *The Story of Philosophy* and concluding with the *Story of Civilization* series.

Despite the sometimes dry turns the book takes, *Philosophy and the Social Problem* still contains glimpses of the Durant literary genius that followed. Imbued with his youthful idealism and his (then) ardent socialistic proclivities, the book is a passionate attempt to remake the world. Even at this early stage, Ariel, his wife and future co-author, was involved

---

1. Durant, Will and Ariel. *A Dual Autobiography*. Simon and Schuster, 1977. p. 71.

in the process, assisting him with the compilation of notes and advising him on certain passages. "I want hammer phrases," she would tell Durant, "sharp and pithy expressions that will concentrate an idea like a blow on the head."[2]

The book was released by the MacMillan Company in the spring of 1917. Sadly, Will Durant's first book failed to ignite the readers' interest. Whereas Durant's later books would be magnificent successes, *Philosophy and the Social Problem* was a magnificent failure, selling a mere 100 copies of its 1,000 copy printing. Alden Freeman, Durant's benefactor (who was also underwriting his university education and providing a stipend for Durant to live on), was forced to cover the cost of the unsold books under the terms of Durant's contract. At MacMillan's request, Durant took possession of the remaining books. He also took his first book's failure in good stride, telling his friends he was in possession of a personal library of over 1,000 books, "nine hundred of which I have written myself."[3]

Despite its initial failure, *Philosophy and the Social Problem* is a book which still deserves to be read. Its arguments are more important today than ever before. With populations increasing and resources dwindling, the complexity of the social problem has never been greater. And philosophy, as an institution, still refuses to acknowledge that it has lost its audience, and that audience must be regained if philosophy hopes to thrive.

James Bishop

---

2. *Ibid.*; p. 72.
3. *Ibid.*; p. 73.

INTRODUCTION

The purpose of this essay is to show: first, that the social problem has been the basic concern of many of the greater philosophers; second, that an approach to the social problem through philosophy is the first condition of even a moderately successful treatment of this problem; and third, that an approach to philosophy through the social problem is indispensable to the revitalization of philosophy.

By "philosophy" we shall understand a study of experience as a whole, or of a portion of experience in relation to the whole.

By the "social problem" we shall understand, simply and very broadly, the problem of reducing human misery by modifying social institutions. It is a problem that, ever reshaping itself, eludes sharper definition; for misery is related to desire, and desire is personal and in perpetual flux: each of us sees the problem unsteadily in terms of his own changing aspirations. It is an uncomfortably complicated problem, of course; and we must bear in mind that the limit of our intention here is to consider philosophy as an approach to the problem, and the problem itself as an approach to philosophy. We are proposing no solutions.

Let us, as a wholesome measure of orientation, touch some of the mountain-peaks in philosophical history, with an eye for the social interest that lurks in every metaphysical maze. "Aristotle," says Professor Woodbridge,[4] "set treatise-writers the fashion of beginning each treatise by reviewing previous opinions on their subject, and proving them all wrong."[5] The purpose of the next five chapters will be rather the opposite: we shall see if some supposedly dead philosophies do not admit of considerable resuscitation. Instead of trying to show that Socrates, Plato, Bacon, Spinoza, and Nietzsche were quite mistaken in their views on the social problem, we shall try to see what there is in these views that can help us to understand our own situation today. We shall not make a collection of systems of social philosophy; we shall not lose ourselves in the past in a scholarly effort to relate each philosophy to its social and political environment; we shall try to relate these philosophies rather to our own environment, to look at our own problems successively through the

---

4. Frederick J. E. Woodbridge, Will Durant's philosophy professor at Colombia University. While Durant studied philosophy at Colombia, Professor Woodbridge served as the Dean of the Faculties of Political Science, Philosophy, and Pure Science. Woodbridge was one of the founders of American Naturalism, a philosophical movement that rejected supernaturalism and embraced the empiricism of science. Elements of American Naturalism are evident throughout this book.

5. Class Lectures. As Bacon has it, Aristotle, after the Ottoman manner, did not believe that he could rule securely unless he first put all his brothers to death.

eyes of these philosophers. Other interpretations of these men we shall not so much contradict as seek to supplement.

Each of our historical chapters, then, will be not so much a review as a preface and a progression. The aim will be neither history nor criticism, but a kind of construction by proxy. It is a method that has its defects: it will, for example, sacrifice thoroughness of scholarship to present applicability, and will necessitate some repetitious gathering of the threads when we come later to our more personal purpose. But as part requital for this, we shall save ourselves from considering the past except as it is really present, except as it is alive and nourishingly significant today. And from each study we shall perhaps make some advance towards our final endeavor - the mutual elucidation of the social problem and philosophy.

PART ONE:
HISTORICAL APPROACH

CHAPTER ONE
THE PRESENT SIGNIFICANCE OF
THE SOCRATIC ETHIC

History as Rebarbarization

History is a process of rebarbarization. A people made vigorous by arduous physical conditions of life, and driven by the increasing exigencies of survival, leaves its native habitat, moves down upon a less vigorous people, conquers, displaces, or absorbs it. Habits of resolution and activity developed in a less merciful environment now rapidly produce an economic surplus; and part of the resources so accumulated serve as capital in a campaign of imperialist conquest. The growing surplus generates a leisure class, scornful of physical activity and adept in the arts of luxury. Leisure begets speculation; speculation dissolves dogma and corrodes custom, develops sensitivity of perception and destroys decision of action. Thought, adventuring in a labyrinth of analysis, discovers behind society the individual; divested of its normal social function it turns inward and discovers the self. The sense of common interest, of commonwealth, wanes; there are no citizens now, there are only individuals.

From afar another people, struggling against the forces of an obdurate environment, sees here the cleared forests, the liberating roads, the harvest of plenty, the luxury of leisure. It dreams, aspires, dares, unites, invades. The rest is as before.

Rebarbarization is rejuvenation. The great problem of any civilization is how to rejuvenate itself without rebarbarization.

Philosophy as Disintegrator

The rise of philosophy, then, often heralds the decay of a civilization. Speculation begins with nature and begets naturalism; it passes to man - first as a psychological mystery and then as a member of society - and begets individualism. Philosophers do not always desire these results; but they achieve them. They feel themselves the unwilling enemies of the state: they think of men in terms of personality, while the state thinks of men in terms of social mechanism. Some philosophers would gladly hold their peace, but there is that in them which will out; and when philosophers speak, gods and dynasties fall. Most states have had their roots in heaven, and have paid the penalty for it: the twilight of the gods is the afternoon of states.

Every civilization comes at last to the point where the individual, made by speculation conscious of himself as an end per se, demands of the state, as the price of its continuance, that it shall henceforth enhance rather than exploit his capacities. Philosophers sympathize with this demand, the state almost always rejects it: therefore civilizations come and civilizations go. The history of philosophy is essentially an account of the efforts great men have made to avert social disintegration by building up natural moral sanctions to take the place of the supernatural sanctions which they themselves have destroyed. To find - without resorting to celestial machinery - some way of winning for their people social coherence and permanence without sacrificing plasticity and individual uniqueness to regimentation, - that has been the task of philosophers, that is the task of philosophers.

We should be thankful that it is. Who knows but that within our own time may come at last the forging of an effective *natural* ethic, an achievement which might be the most momentous event in the history of our world.

Individualism in Athens

The great ages in the history of European thought have been for the most part periods of individualistic effervescence: the age of Socrates, the age of Caesar and Augustus, the Renaissance, the Enlightenment; and shall we add the age which is now coming to a close? These ages have usually been preceded by periods of imperialist expansion: imperialism requires a tightening of the bonds whereby individual allegiance to the state is made secure; and this tightening, given a satiety of imperialism, involves an individualistic reaction. And again, the dissolution of the political or economic frontier by conquest or commerce breaks down cultural barriers between peoples, develops a sense of the relativity of customs, and issues in the opposition of individual "reason" to social tradition.

A political treatise attributed to the fourth century B.C. reflects the attitude that had developed in Athens in the later fifth century. "If all men were to gather in a heap the customs which they hold to be good and noble, and if they were next to select from it the customs which they hold to be base and vile, nothing would be left over."[6] Once such a view- has found capable defenders, the custom-basis of social organization begins to give way, and institutions venerable with age are ruthlessly subpoe-

6. The *Dialexeis*; cf. Gomperz, *Greek Thinkers*, New York, 1901, vol. I, p. 404.

naed to appear before the bar of reason. Men begin to contrast "Nature" with custom, somewhat to the disadvantage of the latter. Even the most basic of Greek institutions is questioned: "The Deity," says a fourth-century Athenian Rousseau, "made all men free; Nature has enslaved no man."[7] Botsford speaks of "the powerful influence of fourth-century socialism on the intellectual class."[8] Euripides and Aristophanes are full of talk about a movement for the emancipation of women.[9] Law and government are examined: Anarcharsis' comparison of the law to a spider's web, which catches small flies and lets the big ones escape, now finds sympathetic comprehension; and men arise, like Callicles and Thrasymachus, who frankly consider government as a convenient instrument of mass-exploitation.

The Sophists

The cultural representatives of this individualistic development were the Sophists. These men were university professors without a university and without the professorial title. They appeared in response to a demand for higher instruction on the part of the young men of the leisure class; and within a generation they became the most powerful intellectual force in Greece. There had been philosophers, questioners, before them; but these early philosophers had questioned nature rather than man or the state. The Sophists were the first group of men in Greece to overcome the natural tendency to acquiesce in the given order of things. They were proud men, - humility is a vice that never found root in Greece, - and they had a buoyant confidence in the newly discovered power of human intelligence. They assumed, in harmony with the spirit of all Greek achievement, that in the development and extension of knowledge lay the road to a sane and significant life, individual and communal; and in the quest for knowledge they were resolved to scrutinize unawed all institutions, prejudices, customs, morals. Protagoras professed to respect conventions,[10] and pronounced conventions and institutions the source of man's superiority to the beast; but his famous principle, that "man is the measure of all things," was a quiet hint that morals are a matter of taste, that we call a man "good" when his conduct is advantageous to us, and "bad" when his conduct threatens to make for our own loss. To the Sophists virtue consisted, not in obedience to unjudged rules and customs, but in the efficient performance of whatever one set out to do. They would have condemned the bungler and let the "sinner" go. That they were flippant

---

7. *Gomperz*, vol. I, p, 403.

8. Botsford and Sibler, *Hellenic Civilization*, New York, 1915, p. 430.

9. *Ibid*,, p, 349, etc.

10. And sincerely, says Burnet, because he had gone through radicalism to skepticism, and felt that one convention was as good as another.

skeptics, putting no distinction of worth between any belief and its oppo-site, and willing to prove anything for a price, is an old accusation which later students of Greek philosophy are almost unanimous in rejecting.[11]

The great discovery of the Sophists was the individual; it was an achievement for which Plato and his oligarchical friends could not forgive them, and because of which they incurred the contumely which it is now so hard to dissociate from their name. The purpose of laws, said the Sophists, was to widen the possibilities of individual development; if laws did not do that, they had better be forgotten. There was a higher law than the laws of men, - a natural law, engraved in every heart, and judge of every other law. The conscience of the individual was above the dictates of any state. All radicalisms lay compact in that pronouncement. Plato, prolific of innovations though he was, yet shrank from such a leap into the new. But the Sophists pressed their point, men listened to them, and the Greek world changed. When Socrates appeared, he found that world all out of joint, a war of all against all, a stridency of uncoordinated person-alities rushing into chaos. And when he was asked, "What should men do to be saved?" he answered, simply, "Let us think."

Intelligence as Virtue

Intelligence as virtue: it was not a new doctrine; it was merely a new emphasis placed on an already important element in the Greek - or rather the Athenian - view of life. But it was a needed emphasis. The Sophists (not Socrates, *pace* Cicero) had brought philosophy down from heaven to earth, but they had left it groveling at the feet of business efficiency and success, a sort of *ancilla pecuniae*, a broker knowing where one's soul could be invested at ten per cent. Socrates agreed with the Sophists in condemning any but a very temporary devotion to metaphysical abstrac-tions, - the one and the many, motion and rest, the indivisibility of space, the puzzles of predication, and so forth; he joined them in ridiculing the pursuit of knowledge for its own sake, and in demanding that all thinking should be focused finally on the real concerns of life; but his spirit was as different from theirs as the spirit of Spinoza was different from that of a medieval moneylender. With the Sophists philosophy was a profession; they were "lovers of wisdom" - for a consideration. With Socrates philos-ophy was a quest of the permanently good, of the lastingly satisfying atti-tude to life. To find out just what are justice, temperance, courage, piety, "that is an inquiry which I shall never be weary of pursuing so far as in me lies." It was not an easy quest; and the results were not startlingly defi-nite: "I wander to and fro when I attempt these problems, and do not

---

11. Cf. Henry Jackson, article "Sophists," *Encyclopedia Britannica*. Eleventh edition.

remain consistent with myself." His interlocutors went from him apparently empty; but he had left in them seed which developed in the after-calm of thought. He could clarify men's notions, he could reveal to them their assumptions and prejudices; but he could not and would not manufacture opinions for them. He left no written philosophy because he had only the most general advice to give, and knew that no other advice is ever taken. He trusted his friends to pass on the good word.

Now what was the good word? It was, first of all, the identity of virtue and wisdom, morals and intelligence; but more than that, it was the basic identity, in the light of intelligence, of communal and individual interests. Here at the Sophist's feet lay the debris of the old morality. What was to replace it? The young Athenians of a generation denuded of supernatural belief would not listen to counsels of "virtue," of self-sacrifice to the community. What was to be done? Should social and political pressure be brought to bear upon the Sophists to compel them to modify the individualistic tenor of their teachings? Analysis destroys morals. What is the moral - destroy analysis?

The moral, answered Socrates, is to get better morals, to find an ethic immune to the attack of the most ruthless skeptic. The Sophists were right, said Socrates; morality means more than social obedience. But the Sophists were wrong in opposing the good of the individual to that of the community; Socrates proposed to prove that if a man were intelligent, he would see that those same qualities which make a man a good citizen - justice, wisdom, temperance, courage - are also the best means to individual advantage and development. All these "virtues" are simply the supreme and only virtue - wisdom - differentiated by the context of circumstance. No action is virtuous unless it is an intelligent adaptation of means to a criticized end. "Sin" is failure to use energy to the best account; it is an unintelligent waste of strength. A man does not knowingly pursue anything but the Good; let him but see his advantage, and he will be attracted towards it irresistibly; let him pursue it, and he will be happy, and the state safe. The trouble is that men lack perspective, and cannot see their true Good; they need not "virtue" but intelligence, not sermons but training in perspective. The man who rules within, who is strong enough to stop and think, the man who has achieved the self knowledge that brings self-command, - such a man will not be deceived by the tragedy of distance, by the apparent smallness of the future good alongside of the more easily appreciable good that lies invitingly at hand. Hence the moral importance of dialectic, of cross-examination, of concept and definition: we must learn "how to make our ideas clear"; we must ask ourselves just what it is that we want, just how real this seeming good is. Dialectic is the handmaiden of virtue; and all clarification is morality.

The Meaning of Virtue

This is frank intellectualism, of course; and the best-refuted doctrine in philosophy. It is amusing to observe the ease with which critics and historians dispatch the Socratic ethic. It is "an extravagant paradox," says Sidgwick,[12] "incompatible with moral freedom." "Nothing is easier," says Gomperz,[13] "than to detect the one-sidedness of this point of view." "This doctrine," says Grote,[14] "omits to notice, what is not less essential, the proper conditions of the emotions, desires, etc." "It tended to make all conduct a matter of the intellect and not of the character, and so in a sense to destroy moral responsibility," says Hobhouse.[15] "Himself blessed with a will so powerful that it moved almost without friction," says Henry Jackson,[16] "Socrates fell into the error of ignoring its operations, and was thus led to regard knowledge as the sole condition of well-doing." "Socrates was a misunderstanding," says Nietzsche;[17] "reason at any price, life made clear, cold, cautious, conscious, without instincts, opposed to the instincts, was in itself only a disease, . . . and by no means a return to 'virtue,' to 'health,' and to 'happiness'." And the worn-out dictum about seeing the better and approving it, yet following the worse, is quoted as the deliverance of a profound psychologist, whose verdict should be accepted as a final solution of the problem.

Before refuting a doctrine it is useful to try to understand it. What could Socrates have meant by saying that all real virtue is intelligence? What is virtue?

A civilization may be characterized in terms of its conception of virtue. There is hardly anything more distinctive of the Greek attitude, as compared with our own, than the Greek notion of virtue as intelligence. Consider the present connotations of the word virtue: men shrink at having the term applied to them; and "nothing makes one so vain," says Oscar Wilde, "as being told that one is a sinner." During the Middle Ages, the official conception of virtue was couched in terms of womanly excellence; and the sternly masculine God of the Hebrews suffered considerably from the inroads of Mariolatry. Protestantism was in part a rebellion

12. *History of Ethics*, London, 1892, p. 24.
13. *Op. cit.*, vol. II, 1905, p. 67.
14. *History of Greece*, vol. VIII, p. 134.
15. *Morals in Evolution*, New York, 1915. p, 556.
16. Henry Jackson, article "Socrates," *Encyclopedia Britannica*, eleventh edition.
17. *Twilight of the Idols*, London, 1915, p. 15. For Nietzsche's answer to Nietzsche, cf. *ibid.*, p, 57: "To accustom the eye to calmness, to patience, and to allow things to come up to it; to defer judgment, and to acquire the habit of approaching and grasping an individual case from all sides, - this is the first preparatory schooling of intellectuality," this is one of "the three objects for which we need educators . . . One must not respond immediately to a stimulus; one must acquire a command of the obstructing and isolating instincts. To learn to see, as I understand this matter, amounts almost to that which in popular language is called 'strength of will': its essential feature is precisely . . . to be able to postpone one's decision . . . All lack of intellectuality, all vulgarity, arises out of the inability to resist a stimulus."

of the ethically subjugated male; in Luther the man emerges riotously from the monk. But as people cling to the ethical implications of a creed long after the creed itself has been abandoned, so our modern notion of virtue is still essentially medieval and feminine. Virginity, chastity, conjugal fidelity, gentility, obedience, loyalty, kindness, self-sacrifice, are the stock-in-trade of all respectable moralists; to be "good" is to be harmless, to be not "bad," to be a sort of sterilized citizen, guaranteed not to injure. This sheepish innocuousness comes easily to the natively uninitiative, to those who are readily amenable to fear and prohibitions. It is a static virtue; it contracts rather than expands the soul; it offers no handle for development, no incentive to social stimulation and productivity. It is time we stopped calling this insipidly negative attitude by the once mighty name of virtue. Virtue must be defined in terms of that which is vitally significant in our lives.

And therefore, too, virtue cannot be defined in terms of individual subordination to the group. The vitally significant thing in a man's life is not the community, but himself. To ask him to consider the interests of the community above his own is again to put up for his worship an external, transcendent god; and the trouble with a transcendent god is that he is sure to be dethroned. To call "immoral" the refusal of the individual to meet such demands is the depth of indecency; it is itself immoral, - that is, it is nonsense. The notion of "duty" as involving self-sacrifice, as essentially duty to others, is a soul-cramping, funereal notion, and deserves all that Ibsen and his progeny have said of it.[18] Ask the individual to sacrifice himself to the community, and it will not be long before he sacrifices the community to himself. Granted that, in the language of Heraclitus, there is always a majority of fools, and that self-sacrifice can be procured by the simple hypnotic suggestion of post-mortem remuneration: sooner or later come doubt and disillusionment, and the society whose permanence was so easily secured becomes driftwood on the tides of time. History means that if it means anything.

No; the intelligent individual will give allegiance to the group of which he happens to find himself a member, only so far as the policies of the group accord with his own criticized desires. Whatever allegiance he offers will be to those forces, wherever they may be, which in his judgment move in the line of these desires. Even for such forces he will not sacrifice himself, though there may be times when martyrdom is a luxury for which life itself is not too great a price. Since these forces have been defined in terms of his own judgment and desire, conflict between them and himself can come only when his behavior diverges from the purposes defined and resumed in times of conscious thought, - *i.e.*, only when

---

18. "Why art thou sad? Assuredly thou hast performed some sacred duty?" - Basarov in Turgenev's *Father and Children*, 1903. p. 185.

he ceases to adapt means to his ends, ceases, that is, to be intelligent. The prime moral conflict is not between the individual and his group, but between the partial self of fragmentary impulse and the coordinated self of conscious purpose. There is a group within each man as well as without: a group of partial selves is the reality behind the figment of the unitary self. Every individual is a society, every person is a crowd. And the tragedies of the moral life lie not in the war of each against all, but in the restless interplay of these partial selves behind the stage of action. As a man's intelligence grows this conflict diminishes, for both means and ends, both behavior and purposes, are being continually revised and redirected in accordance with intelligence, and therefore in convergence towards it. Progressively the individual achieves unity, and through unity, personality. Faith in himself has made him whole. The ethical problem, so far as it is the purely individual problem of attaining to coordinated personality, is solved.

Moral responsibility, then, - whatever social responsibility may be - is the responsibility of the individual to himself. The social is not necessarily the moral - let the sociological fact be what it will. The unthinking conformity of the "normal social life" is, just because it is unthinking, below the level of morality: let us call it sociality, and make morality the prerogative of the really thinking animal. In any society so constituted as to give to the individual an increase in powers as recompense for the pruning of his liberties, the unsocial will be immoral - that is, self-destructively unreasonable and unintelligent; but even in such a society the moral would overflow the margins of the social, and would take definition ultimately from the congruity of the action with the criticized purposes of the individual self. This does not mean that all ethics lies compact in the shibboleth, "Be yourself." Those who make the least sparing use of this phrase are too apt to consider it an excuse for lives that reek with the heat of passion and smack of insufficient evolution. These people need to be reminded all the more forcibly since the most palatable and up-to-date philosophies exalt instinct and deride thought - that one cannot be thoroughly one's self except by deliberation and intelligence. To act indeliberately is not to be, but in great part to cancel, one's self. For example, the vast play of direct emotional expression is almost entirely indeliberate: if you are greatly surprised, your lips part, your eyes open a trifle wider, your pulse quickens, your respiration is affected; and if I am surprised, though you be as different from me as Hyperion from a satyr, my respiration will be affected, my pulse will quicken, my eyes will open a trifle wider, and my lips will part - my direct reaction will be essentially the same as yours. The direct expression of surprise is practically the same in all the higher animals. Darwin's classical description of the expression of fear is another example; it holds for every normal human being, not to speak of lower species. So with egotism, jealousy, anger, and a thousand other instinctive reaction-complexes, they are common to the species, and when we so react, we are expressing not our individual selves so much as the species to which we happen to belong. When you hit a man because he has "insulted" you, when you swagger a little after delivering a successful speech, when you push aside women and children in order to take their place in the rescue boat, when you do anyone of a million indeliberate things like these, it is not you that acts, it is your species, it is your ancestors, acting through you; your acquired individual difference is lost in the whirlwind of inherited impulse. Your act, as the Scholastics phrased it, is not a "human" act; you yourself are not really acting in any full measure of yourself, you are but playing slave and mouthpiece to the dead. But subject the inherited tendencies to the scrutiny of your individual experience, *think*, and your action will then express yourself, not in any abbreviated sense, but up to the hilt. There is no merit, no "virtue," no development in playing the game of fragmentary impulses, in living up to the past; to be moral, to grow, is to be not part but all of one's self, to call into operation the acquired as well as the inherited elements of one's character, to be *whole*. So many of us invite ruin by actions which do not really express us, but are the voice of the merest fragment of ourselves, - the remainder of us being meanwhile asleep.[19] To be whole, to be your deliberate self, to do what you please but only after considering what you really please, to follow your own ideals (but to follow them I), to choose your own means and not to have them forced upon you by your ancestors, to act consciously, to see the part *sub specie totius*, to see the present act in its relation to your vital purposes, to think, to be intelligent, - all these are definitions of virtue and morality.

There is, then, in the old sense of the word, no such thing as morality, there is only intelligence or stupidity. Yes, virtue is calculus, horrible as that may sound to long and timid ears: to calculate properly just what you must do to attain your real ends, to see just what and where your good is, and to make for it - that is all that can without indecency be asked of any man, that is all that is ever vouchsafed by any man who is intelligent.

Perhaps you think it is an easy virtue, - this cleaving to intelligence, - easier than being harmless. Try it.

"Instinct" and "Reason"

And now to go back to the refutations.

The strongest objection to the Socratic doctrine is that intelligence is not a creator, but only a servant, of ends. What we shall consider to be

---

19. "Morality is the effort to throw off sleep . . . I have never yet met a man who was wide awake. How could I have looked him in the face?" - Thoreau, *Walden*, New York, 1899, p. 92.

our good appears to be determined not by reason, but by desire. Reason itself seems but the valet of desire, ready to do for it every manner of menial service. Desire is an adept at marshalling before intelligence such facts as favor the wish, and turns the mind's eye resolutely away from other truth, as a magician distracts the attention of his audience while his hands perform their wonders. If morality is entirely a matter of intelligence, it is entirely a question of means, it is excluded irrevocably from the realm of ends.

The conclusion may be allowed in substance, though it passes beyond the warrant of the facts. It is true that basic ends are never suggested by intelligence, reason, knowledge; but it is also true that many ends suggested by desire are vetoed by intelligence. Why are the desires of a man more modest than those of a boy or a child, if not because the blows of repeated failure have dulled the edge of desire? Desires lapse, or lose in stature, as knowledge grows and man takes lessons from reality. There is an adaptation of ends to means as well as of means to ends; and desire comes at last to take counsel of its slave.

Be it granted, nonetheless, that ends are dictated by desire, and that if morality is intelligence, there can be no question of the morality of any end *per se*. That, strangely, is not a refutation of the Socratic ethic so much as an essential element of it and its starting-point. Every desire has its own initial right; morality means not the suppression of desires, but their coordination. What that implies for society we shall see presently, for the individual it implies that he is immoral, not when he seeks his own advantage, but when he does not really behave for his own advantage, when some narrow temporary purpose upsets perspective and overrides a larger end.[20] What we call "self-control" is the permanent predominance of the larger end; what we call weakness of will is instability of perspective. Self-control means an intelligent judgment of values, an intelligent coordination of motives, an intelligent forecasting of effects. It is far-sight, far-hearing, an enlargement of the sense; it hears the weakened voice of the admonishing past, it sees results far down the vista of the future; it annihilates space and time for the sake of light. Self-control is coordinated energy, which is the first and last word in ethics and politics, and perhaps in logic and metaphysics too. Weak will means that desires fall out of focus, and taking advantage of the dark steal into action: it is a derangement of the light, a failure of intelligence. In this sense a "good will" means coordination of desires by the ultimate desire, end, ideal; it means health and wholeness of will; it means, literally, integrity. In the old

---

20. What happens when I "see the better and approve it, but follow the worse," is that an end later approved as "better" - *i.e.*, better for me - is at the time obscured by the persistent or recurrent suggestion of an end temporarily more satisfying, but eventually disappointing. Most self-reproach is the use of knowledge won post factum to criticize a self that had to adventure into action unarmed with this hindsight wisdom.

sense "good will" meant, too often, mere fear either of the prohibitions of present law or of the prohibitions stored up in conscience. Such conscience, we all know, is a purely negative and static thing, a convenient substitute for policemen, a degenerate descendant of that *conscientia*, or *knowing-together*, which meant to the Romans a discriminating awareness in action, - discriminating awareness of the whole that lurks round the corner of every part. This is one instance of a sort of pathology of words - words coming to function in a sense alien to their normal intent. *Right* and *wrong*, for example, once carried no ethical connotation, but merely denoted a direct or tortuous route to a goal; and significantly the Hebrew word for sin meant, in the days of its health, an arrow that had missed its mark.

But, it is urged, there is no such thing as intelligence in the sense of a control of passion by reason, desire by thought. Granted; it is so much easier to admit objections than to refute them! Let intelligence be interpreted as you will, so be it you recognize in it a delayed response, a moment of reprieve before execution, giving time for the appearance of new impulses, motives, tendencies, and allowing each element in the situation to fall into its place in a coordinated whole. Let intelligence be a struggle of impulses, a survival of the fittest desire; let us contrast not reason with passion, but response delayed by the rich interplay of motive forces, with response immediately following upon the first-appearing impulse. Let impulse mean for us fruit that falls unripe from the tree, because too weak to hang till it is mature. Let us understand intelligence as not a faculty superadded to impulse, but rather that coordination of impulses which is wrought out by the blows of hard experience. The Socratic ethic fits quite comfortably into this scheme; intelligence is delayed response, and morality means, Take your time.

It is charged that the Socratic view involves determinism; and this charge, too, is best met with open-armed admission. We need not raise the question of the pragmatic value of the problem. But to suppose that determinism destroys moral responsibility is to betray the mid-Victorian origin of one's philosophy. Men of insight like Socrates, Plato, and Spinoza, saw without the necessity of argument that moral responsibility is not a matter of freedom of will, but a relation of means to ends, a responsibility of the agent to himself, an intelligent coordination of impulses by one's ultimate purposes. Any other morality, whatever pretty name it may display, is the emasculated morality of slaves.

The Secularization of Morals

The great problem involved in the Socratic ethic lies, apparently, in the bearings of the doctrine on social unity and stability. Apparently; for it is wholesome to remember that social organization, like the Sabbath, was made for man, and not the other way about. If social organization demands of the individual more sacrifices than its advantages are worth to him, then the stability of that organization is not a problem, it is a misfortune. But if the state does not demand such sacrifices, the advantage of the individual will be in social behavior; and the question whether he will behave socially becomes a question of how much intelligence he has, how clear-eyed he is in ferreting out his own advantage. In a state that does not ask more from its members than it gives, morality and intelligence and social behavior will not quarrel. The social problem appears here as the twofold problem of, first, making men intelligent, and, second, making social organization so great an advantage to the individual as to insure social behavior in all intelligent men.

Which has the better chance of survival: a society of "good" men or a society of intelligent men? So far as a man is "good" he merely obeys, he does not initiate. A society of "good" men is necessarily stagnant; for in such a society the virtue most in demand, as Emerson puts it, is conformity. If great men emerge through the icy crust of this conformity, they are called criminals and sinners; the lives of great men all remind us that we cannot make our lives sublime and yet be "good." But intelligence as an ethical ideal is a progressive norm; for it implies the progressive coordination of one's life in reference to one's ultimate ideals. The god of the "good" man is the status quo; the intelligent man obeys rather the call of the *status ad quem.*

Observe how the problem of man versus the group is clarified by thus relating the individual to a larger whole determined not by geographical frontiers, but by purposes born of his own needs and molded by his own intelligence. For as the individual's intelligence grows, his purposes are brought more and more within the limits of personal capacity and social possibility: he is ever less inclined to make unreasonable demands upon himself, or men in general, or the group in which he lives. His ever-broadening vision makes apparent the inherent self-destructiveness of antisocial aims; and though he chooses his ends without reference to any external moral code, those ends are increasingly social. Enlightenment saves his social dispositions from groveling conformity, and his "self-regarding sentiments" from suicidal narrowness. And now the conflict between himself and his group continues for the most part only in so far as the group makes unreasonable demands upon him. But this, too, diminishes as the individuals constituting or dominating the group become themselves more intelligent, more keenly cognizant of the limits within which the demands of the group upon its members must be restricted if individual allegiance is to be retained. Since the reduction of the conflict between the individual and the community without detriment to the interests of either is the central problem of political ethics, it is obvious that the practical task of ethics is not to formulate a specific moral code, but to bring about a spread of intelligence. And since the reduction of this conflict brings with it a better coordination of the members of the group, through their greater ability to perceive the advantages of communal action in an intelligently administered group, the problem of social coherence and permanence itself falls into the same larger problem of intellectual development.

How to make our ideas clear - what if that be the social problem? What a wealth of import in that little phrase of Socrates, - "what is it?" What is my good, my interest? What do I really want? - To find the answer to that, said Robert Louis Stevenson, is to achieve wisdom and old age. What is my country? What is patriotism? "If you wish to converse with me," said Voltaire, "you must define your terms." If you wish to be moral, you must define your terms. If our civilization is to keep its head above the flux of time, we must define our terms.

For these are the critical days of the secularization of moral sanctions; the theological navel string binding men to "good behavior" has snapped.[21] What are the leaders of men going to do about it? Will they try again the old gospel of self-sacrifice? But a world fed on self-sacrifice is a world of lies, a world choking with the stench of hypocrisy. To preach self-sacrifice is not to solve, it is precisely to shirk, the problem of ethics - the problem of eliminating individual self-sacrifice while preserving social stability: the problem of reconciling the individual as such with the individual as citizen. Or will our leaders try to replace superstition with an extended physical compulsion, making the policeman and the prison do all the work of social coordination? But surely compulsion is a last resort; not because it is "wrong," but because it is inexpedient, because it rather cuts than unties the knot, because it produces too much friction to allow of movement. Compulsion is warranted when there is question of preventing the interference of one individual or group with another; but it is a poor instrument for the establishment or maintenance of ideals. Suppose we stop moralizing, suppose we reduce regimentation, suppose we begin to define our terms. Suppose we let people know quite simply (and not in Academese) that moral codes are born not in heaven but in social needs;

---

21. One of the chief tenets of Will Durant's philosophical perspective was his belief that religion was necessary for the development and maintenance of civilization. As Durant wrote: "Our instincts were formed during a thousand centuries of insecurity and the chase; they fit us to be violent hunters and voracious polygamists rather than peaceable citizens; their once necessary vigor exceeds present social need; they must be checked a hundred times a day, consciously or not, to make society and civilization possible. Families and states, from ages before history, have enlisted the aid of religion to moderate the barbarous impulses of men. Parents found religion helpful in taming the willful child to modesty and self-restraint; educators valued it as a precious means of disciplining and refining youth; governments long since sought its cooperation in forging social order out of the disruptive egoism and natural anarchism of men. If religion had not existed, the great legislators -- Hammurabi, Moses, Lycurgus, Numa Pompilius -- would have invented it." (Source: www.willdurant.com/religion.htm)

and suppose we set about finding a way of spreading intelligence so that individual treachery to real communal interest, and communal exploitation of individual allegiance, may both appear on the surface, as they are at bottom, unintelligently suicidal. Is that too much to hope for? Perhaps. But then again, it may be, the worth and meaning of life lie precisely in this, that there is still a possibility of organizing that experiment.

"Happiness" and "Virtue"

A word now about the last part of the Socratic formula: intelligence = virtue = happiness. And this a word of warning: remember that the "virtue" here spoken of is not the medieval virtue taught in Sunday schools. Surely our children must wonder are we fools or liars when we tell them, "Be good and you will be happy." Better forget "virtue" and read simply: intelligence = happiness. That appears more closely akin to the rough realities of life: intelligence means ability to adapt means to ends, and happiness means success in adapting means to ends; happiness, then, varies with ability. Happiness is intelligence on the move; a pervasive physiological tonus accompanying the forward movement of achievement. It is not the consciousness of virtue: that is not happiness, but snobbery. And similarly, remorse is, in the intelligent man, not the consciousness of "sin," but the consciousness of a past stupidity. So far as you fail to win your real ends you are unhappy - and have proved unintelligent. But the Preacher says, "He that increaseth knowledge increaseth sorrow." True enough if the increment of knowledge is the correction of a past error; the sorrow is a penalty paid for the error, not for the increase of knowledge. True, too, that intelligence does not consistently lessen conflicts, and that it discloses a new want for every want it helps to meet. But the joy of life lies not so much in the disappearance of difficulties as in the overcoming of them; not so much in the diminution of conflict as in the growth of achievement. Surely it is time we had an ethic that stressed achievement rather than quiescence. And further, intelligence must not be thought of as the resignation of disillusionment, the consciousness of impotence; intelligence is to be conceived of in terms of adaptive activity, of movement towards an end, of coordinated self-expression and behavior. Finally, it is but fair to interpret the formula as making happiness and intelligence coincide only so far as the individual's happiness depends on his own conduct. The causes of unhappiness may be an inherited deformity, or an accident not admitting of provision; such cases do not so much contradict as lie outside the formula. So far as your happiness depends on your activities, it will vary with the degree of intelligence you show. Act intelligently, and you will not know regret; feel that you are moving on toward your larger ends, and you will be happy.

The Socratic Challenge

But if individual and social health and happiness depend on intelligence rather than on "virtue," and if the exaltation of intelligence was a cardinal element in the Athenian view of life, why did the Socratic ethic fail to save Athens from decay? And why did the supposedly intelligent Athenians hail this generous old Dr. Johnson of philosophy into court and sentence him to death?

The answer is because the Athenians refused to make the Socratic experiment. They were intelligent, but not intelligent enough. They could diagnose the social malady, could trace it to the decay of supernatural moral norms; but they could not find a cure, they had not the vision to see that salvation lay not in the compulsory retention of old norms, but in the forging of new and better ones, capable of withstanding the shock of questioning and trial. What they saw was chaos; and like most statesmen they longed above all things for order. They were not impressed by Socrates' allegiance to law, his cordial admission of the individual's obligations to the community for the advantages of social organization. They listened to the disciples: to Antisthenes, who laughed at patriotism; to Aristippus, who denounced all government; to Plato, scorner of democracy; and they attacked the master because (not to speak of pettier political reasons) it was he, they thought, who was the root of the evil. They could not see that this man was their ally and not their foe; that rescue for Athens lay in helping him rather than in sentencing him to die. And how well they could have helped him! For to preach intelligence is not enough; there remains to provide for every one the instrumentalities of intelligence. What men needed, what Athenian statesmanship might have provided, was an organization of intelligence for intelligence, an organization of all the forces of intelligence in the state in a persistent intellectual campaign. If that could not save Athens, Athens could not be saved. But the myopic leaders of the Athenian state could not see salvation in intelligence, they could only see it in hemlock. And Socrates had to die.

It will take a wise courage to accept the Socratic challenge, - such courage as battlefields and senate chambers are not wont to show. But unless that wise courage comes to us our civilization will go as other civilizations have come and gone, "kindled and put out like a flame in the night."

NOTE - From a book whose interesting defense of the Socratic ethic from the standpoint of psychoanalysis was brought to the writer's attention after the completion of the foregoing essay: "The Freudian ethics is a literal and concrete justification of the Socratic teaching. Truth is the sole moral sanction, and discrimination of hitherto unrealized facts is the one way out of every moral dilemma . . . Virtue is wisdom." Practical morality is "the establishment, through discrimination, of consistent, and not contradictory (mutually suppressive), courses of action toward phenomena. The moral sanction lies always in facts presented by the phenomena; morality in the discrimination of those facts." Moral development is "the progressive, lifelong integration of experience." - The Freudian Wish and Its Place in Ethics, *by Edwin B. Holt, New York, 1915, pp, 141, 145, 148.*

CHAPTER TWO
PLATO: PHILOSOPHY AS POLITICS

The Man and the Artist

Why do we love Plato? Perhaps because Plato himself was a lover: lover of comrades, lover of the sweet intoxication of dialectical revelry, full of passion for the elusive reality behind thoughts and things. We love him for his unstinted energy, for the wildly nomadic play of his fancy, for the joy which he found in life in all its unredeemed and adventurous complexity. We love him because he was alive every minute of his life, and never ceased to grow; such a man can be loved even for the errors he has made. But above all we love him because of his high passion for social reconstruction through intelligent control; because he retained throughout his eighty years that zeal for human improvement which is for most of us the passing luxury of youth; because he conceived philosophy as an instrument not merely for the interpretation, but for the remolding, of the world. He speaks of himself, through Socrates, as "almost the only Athenian living who sets his hand to the true art of politics; I am the only politician of my time."[22] Philosophy was for him a study of human possibilities in the light of human realities and limitations; his daily food consisted of the problems of human relations and endeavors: problems of liberty versus order; of sex relations and the family; of ideals of character and citizenship, and the educational approaches to those ideals; problems of the control of population, of heredity and environment, of art and morals. With all his liking for the poetry of mysticism, philosophy none the less was to him preeminently an adventure in this world; and unlike ourselves, who follow one or another of his many leads, he sailed virginal seas. Every reader in every age has called him modern; but what age can there be to which Plato will not still be modern?

Plato was twenty-eight when Socrates died;[23] and though he was not present at the drinking of the hemlock, yet the passing of the master must have been a tragic blow to him. It brought him face to face with death, the mother of metaphysics. Proudest of all philosophers, he did not hide his sense of debt to Socrates: "I thank the gods," he said, "that I was born freeman, not slave; Greek, not barbarian; man, not woman; but above all

---

22. *Gorgias*, p. 521.
23. 399 B.C.

that I was born in the time of Socrates." The old philosopher gone, Athens became for a time intolerable to Plato (some say, Plato to Athens), and the young philosopher sailed off to see foreign shores and take nourishment of other cultures. He liked the peaceful orderliness and aged dignity with which a long dominant priesthood had invested Egypt; beside this mellow civilization, he was willing to be told, the culture of his native Athens was but a precarious ethnological sport. He liked the Pythagoreans of southern Italy, with their aristocratic approach to the problem of social construction and their communal devotion to plain living and high thinking; above all he liked their emphasis on harmony as the fundamental pervasive relation of all things and as the ideal in which our human discords might be made to resolve themselves had men artistry enough. Other lands he saw and learned from: stories tell how he risked his handsome head to build an ideal state in Syracuse; how he was sold into slavery and redeemed by a friend; and how he passed down through Palestine even to India, absorbing the culture of their peoples with a kind of osmotic genius. And at last, after twelve years of wandering, he heard again the call of Athens, and went home, stored with experience and ripe with thought.

Arrived now at the mid-point of his life, he turned to the task of self-expression. Should he join one of the political parties and try to make the government of Athens a picture of his thought? Perhaps he felt that his thought was not yet definite enough for that; politics requires answers in Yes or No, and philosophy deals only in Yes *and* No. He hesitated to join a party or pledge himself to a dogma; and was prepared to be hated by all parties alike for this hesitation.[24] Aristocracy was in his blood, and he would not stoop to conquer by a plebiscite. He thought of turning to the stage, as Euripides had done, and teaching through the mask; in his youth he had written plays, and smiled now to think how he had hoped to rival Aristophanes. But there were too many limitations here, of religious subject and dramatic form; Plato's philosophy was a thing of ever broadening borders, and could not be cramped into a ceremony. But neither was his philosophy an arid academic affair, to be written down as one places in order the bones of a skeleton; it was vibrantly alive, it was itself a drama and a religion. Why should there not be a drama of idea as well as of action? Had not the play of thought its tragedies and comedies? Was not philosophy, after all, a matter of life and death?

In such a juncture of desires came that fusion of drama and philosophy which we know as Plato's dialogues, - assuredly the finest production in all the history of philosophy. Here was just the instrument for a man whose thought had not congealed into dogmas and a system. All genius is heterogeneous; a great man is a sum of many men - let the soul give

---

24. *Epistles.* VIII. 325.

its selves a voice, and it will speak in dialogue.[25] Just instrument, too, for a man who wished to play with the varied possibilities of speculation, who cared to clarify his own mind rather than to give forth finalities where life itself was so blind and inconclusive. A conclusion is too often but the point at which thought has lost its wind; being not so much a solution of the problem as a dissolution of thought. Hence the riotous play of the imagination in Plato; lively game of trial and error, merry-go-round of thought; here is imagery squandered with lordly abandon; here is humor such as one misses in our ponderous modern philosophers; here is no system but all systems;[26] here is one abounding fountainhead of European thought; here is prose strong and beautiful as the great temples where Greek joy disported itself in marble; here literary prose is born - and born adult.

Bow to Solve the Social Problem

To understand Plato one must remember the Pythagorean motif: harmony is the heart of Plato's metaphysics, of his psychological and educational theory, of his ethics and his politics. To feel such harmony as there is, and to make such harmony as may be - that to Plato is the meaning of philosophy.

We observe this at the outset in the more mystified-than mystifying theory of ideas. Obviously, the theory of ideas belongs to Socrates; the Platonic element is a theory not of ideas so much as of ideals. Socrates wants truth, but Plato wants beauty, harmony. Socrates is bent on argument, and points you to a concept; Plato is a poet with a vision, and points you to the picture that he sees. Understanding, says Plato, is of the earth earthly; but poetic vision is divine![27] Hence the maze of quibbling in the dialogues; it is Plato and not Socrates who is culprit here. Reasoning was an alien art to Plato; try as he might to become a mathematician he remained always a poet - and perhaps most so when he dealt with numbers. Dialectic was in Plato's day a recent invention; he plays with it like a youth in the breakers, letting it now raise him to heights of ecstatic vision and now bury him in the deadliest logic-chopping. But - let us not doubt it - he knows when he is logic-chopping; he goes on, partly that he may paint his picture, partly for the mere joy of parrying pros and cons; this new game, he feels, is a sport for the gods.

Let us smile at the heavy seriousness of those who suppose that this man meant everything he said. No one does, but least of all men Plato, who hardly taught except in parables. What is the "heaven" of the ideas but a poet's way of saying that the constancies observable in the relations

---

25. "When the soul does not speak in dialogue it is not in difficulty." - Professor Woodbridge, in class.
26. "If we look for a system of philosophy in Plato, we shall probably not find it; but if we look for none we may find most of the philosophies ever written." - Professor Woodbridge.
27. *Phaedrus*, 244.

among things are not identical with the things themselves, but have a reality and permanence of their own? So we phrase it in our own distinguished verbiage; but Plato prefers, as ever, to draw a picture. And notice, in this picture, the ever-present reference to social needs. What is a concept, after all, but a scheme for the conservation of mental resources, an instrument of prediction, a method of control? Without the power to form concepts we could never turn experience to use, it would slip between our fingers; we should be like the maidens condemned to carry water in a sieve. The *idea* of anything is the sum of its observed constancies of behavior; hence the medium of our adaptation and control. To have *ideas* of things is to know the map or plan of things; it is to see tendencies, directions, and results; it is to know how to use things. That is why knowledge is power; every idea is a tool with which to bend the world to serve our will. And that too is why the Ideas are real: they have power, and "anything which possesses any sort of power is real."[28]

All this, as was said, is but an embellishment of the Socratic doctrine that salvation lies in brains. But Plato rushes on. Not only may everything be brought under a concept, an Idea, but it may be brought under a perfect Form, an Ideal. Things are not what they might be. Men are not such as men might be, states are often sorry states, beds might be more ideal beds, even dirt could be more perfectly dirt. To all things that are, there correspond perfect Ideals of what they might be, in a thoroughly harmonious world. To say that these Ideals are real, that they exist, is only to claim for them that they are operative and get results. Whether his supernaturalism was only part of his political theory, others may dispute; let it suffice us at present that Plato believed that the Ideals could and did operate through human agency. The distinctive thing about man is that perceiving the thing that is, he can conceive the thing that might be. He is the forward-looking, ideal-making animal; through him, if he but will it, proceeds creation. The brute may be a thinker, but man may be also an artist. Out of the abundance of the sexual instinct (as Plato implies in the *Symposium*) emerges this ideal-seeking and making quality, from which come art and ethics and religion. William Morris looks at a slum and conceives Utopia; and forthwith begins to make for Utopia even though the road leads him through a jail. Is it that William Morris loves "humanity"? Not at all; he loves beauty and his dream; he is uncomfortable with all this dirt and despair before him; it is his fortune or misfortune that he cannot see these slums without falling thrall to a vision of better things. So with most of us "reformers": we wish to change things, not because we love our fellows much more than "conservatives" do, nor because we believe that happiness varies with income, but because we hear the call of the beautiful, and see in the mind's eye another form wherein the world might

---

28. *Sophist*, 247.

come more pleasingly to sight.

What we have to do, says Plato, is to make people conceive a better world, so that they may see this world as ugly, and may strive to reshape it. We must conceive the perfect Forms of things, and batter this poor world till it reforms itself and take these perfect shapes. To learn to see - and seeing learn to make - these perfect Forms: that is the task of philosophers. To make philosophers: that is the social problem.

On Making Philosopher-Kings

It is simple, isn't it? Give us enough philosophers, and the beautiful city will walk out of the picture into the fact. But how make philosophers? And perhaps there is a perfect Form for philosophers, too? How shall we "see - and seeing learn to make" - the perfect philosopher?

Let us not worry about this little matter of dialectics, says Plato; we know quite well some of the things we must do in order that we may have more and greater philosophers. It is quite clear that one thing we must do is to give our best brains to education.

Is that trite? Not at all. Do we give our best brains to education? Do we offer more to our ministers or commissioners of education than to our presidents, or governors, or mayors, or bank presidents, or pugilists? Or do we honor them more? When Plato says that the office of minister of education is "of all the great offices of state the greatest," and that the citizens should elect their very best man to this office,[29] he is not pronouncing a platitude, he is making a radical, a revolutionary proposition, It has never been done, and it will not soon be done; for men, naturally enough, are more interested in making money than in making philosophers. And yet, says Plato, gently but resolutely, we may as well understand that until we give our best brains to the problem of making philosophers our much-ado about social ills will amount to noise and wind, and nothing more. "How charming people are I," he writes, drawing an analogy between the individual and the body politic, "they are always doctoring - and thereby increasing and complicating - their disorders, fancying they will be cured by some nostrum which somebody advises them to try, never getting better but always growing worse . . . Are they not as good as a play, trying their hand at legislation, and imagining that by reforms they will make an end to the dishonesties and rascalities of mankind, not knowing that they are in reality cutting away at the heads of a hydra?"[30]

Notice that the aim of the educational process is, for Plato, not so much the general spread of intelligence as the discovery and development of the superior man. (This conception of the task of the educator

---

29. *Laws*, 765-6.
30. *Republic*, 425.

appears again and again in later thought: we hear it in the nineteenth century, for example, in Carlyle's "hero," Schopenhauer's "genius," and Nietzsche's "superman.") It is very naive, thinks Plato, to look to the masses as the source and hope of social improvement; the proper function of the masses is to toil as cheerfully as may be for the development and support of the genius who will make them happy - so far as they are capable of happiness. To aim directly at the elevation of all is to open the door to mediocrity and futility; to find and nurse the potential genius - that is an end worthy of the educator's subtle art.

Now if you are going to discover genius in the bud you must above all things handle your material, at the outset at least, with tender care. You must not overflow with prohibitions, or indulge yourself too much in the luxury of punishments. "Mother and father and nurse and tutor set to quarrelling about the improvement of the child as soon as ever he is able to understand them: he cannot say or do anything without their setting forth to him that this is just and that unjust, this honorable and that dishonorable, this holy and that unholy, do this and don't do that. And if he obeys, well and good; if not, he is straightened by threats and blows, like a piece of warped wood."[31] Suppress here, and you get expression there - often enough, abnormal expression. Better have no hard mold of uniformity and conformity wherein to crush and deform each differently aspiring soul. Think twice before forcing your 'isms and 'ologies upon the child; his own desires will be your best curriculum. "The elements of instruction," writes Plato, in a too little-noticed passage, "should be presented to the mind in childhood, but without any notion of forcing them. For a freeman ought to be a freeman in the acquisition of knowledge. Bodily exercise, when compulsory, does no harm, but knowledge (which is acquired under compulsion) has no hold on the mind. Therefore do not use compulsion, but let early education be a sort of amusement that will better enable you to find out the natural bent."[32] There is a stroke of Plato's genius here: it is a point which we laggards are coming to after some two thousand three hundred years. "To find out the natural bent," to catch the spark of divine fire before conformity can put it out; that is the beginning and yet the summit of the educator's task - the *initium dimidium facti*.

In this search for genius all souls shall be tried. Education must be universal and compulsory; children belong not to parents but to the state and to the future.[33] And education cannot begin too early. Cleinias, asking whether education should begin at birth, is astonished to be answered, "No, before"; and if Plato could have his way, no doubt there would be a realization of Dr. Holmes' suggestion that a man's education

31. *Protagoras*, 325.
32. *Republic*, 536.
33. *Laws*, 804.

should begin two thousand years before he is born. The chief concern at the outset will be to develop the body, and not to fill the soul with letters; let the child be taught his letters at ten, but not before.[34] Music will share with gymnastics the task of rounded development. The boy who tells his teacher that the athletic field is as important and necessary a part of education as the lecture room is right. "How shall we find a gentle nature which has also great courage?"[35] Music mixed with athletics will do it. "I am quite aware that your mere athlete becomes too much of a savage, and that the musician is melted and softened beyond what is good for him."[36] There is a determination here that even the genius shall be healthy; Plato will not tolerate the notion that to be a genius one needs to be sick: let the genius have his say, but let him, too, be reminded that he is no disembodied spirit. And let art take care lest its vaunted purgation be a purgation of our strength and manhood; poetry and soft music may make men slaves. No man shall bother with music after the age of sixteen.[37]

At twenty a general test will weed out those who give indication that further educative labor will be wasted on them; the others will go on for another decade, and a second test will eliminate those who will in the meantime have reached the limit of their capacities for development. The final survivors will then - and not before - be introduced to philosophy. "They must not be allowed to taste the dear delight too early; that is a thing especially to be avoided; for young men, as you may have observed, when they first get the taste in their mouths, argue for amusement, and are always contradicting and refuting, like puppy-dogs that delight to tear and pull at all who come near them . . . And when they have made many conquests and received defeats at the hands of many, they violently and speedily get into a way of not believing anything that they believed before, and hence not only they, but philosophy generally, have a bad name with the rest of the world."[38]

Five happy years are given to the study of philosophy. Gradually, the student learns to see the universal behind the particular, to judge the part by relating it to the whole; the fragments of his experience fall into a harmonious philosophy of life. The sciences which he has learned are now united as a consistent application of intelligence to life; indeed, the faculty of uniting the sciences and focusing them on the central problems of life, is precisely the criterion of the true philosopher.[39] But involved in this is a certain practical quality, a sense for realities and limitations. One must

---

34. *Ibid.*, 810.
35. *Republic*, 375.
36. *Ibid.*, 410.
37. *Laws*, 810.
38. *Republic*, 539.
39. *Republic*, 537.

study books - and men; one should read much, but live more. So Plato legislates that his new philosophers shall spend the years from thirty-five to fifty in the busy din of practical life; they must, in his immortal image, go back into the cave. The purpose of higher education is to detach us for a time from the life of action, but only so that we may later return to it with a better perspective. To be put for a goodly time upon one's own resources, to butter one's own bread for a while, - that is an almost indispensable prerequisite to greatness. Out of such a test men come with the scars of many wounds; but to those who are not fools every scar is the mark of a lesson learned.

And now here are our philosophers, ripe and fifty, hardened by the tests of learning and of life. What shall we do with them? Put them away in a lecture-room and pay no further attention to them? Give them, as their life work, the problem of finding how Spinoza deduces, or fails to deduce, the Many from the One? Have them fill learned esoteric journals with unintelligible jargon about the finite and the infinite, or space and time, or the immateriality of roast beef? No, says Plato; let them govern the state.

Did Plato mean it? Was he so enraged at the state-murder of the most beloved of philosophers that he forearmed himself against such a *contretemps* in his Utopia by making the philosophers supreme? Was it only his magnificent journalistic revenge? Was it merely his reaction to the observed cramping and mediocritization of superior intellects in a democracy? Was it but Plato's dramatic way of emphasizing the Socratic plea for intelligence as the basis of morals and social life? Perhaps *all* this, but much more. It was his sober judgment; it was the influence of the Egyptian priesthood and the Pythagorean brotherhood coming to the surface in him; it was the long-accumulated deposit of the stream of his personal experience.

We have to remember here that by philosopher Plato does not mean Immanuel Kant. He means a living being, a man like Seneca or Francis Bacon, a man in whom knowledge is fused with action, and keen perception joins with steady hand; a man who has had not only the teaching of books but the discipline of hard experience; a man who has learned with equal readiness to obey and to command; a man whose thought is coordinated by application to the vital problems of human society. "Inasmuch as philosophers alone are able to grasp the eternal and unchangeable, and those who wander in the region of the many and variable are not philosophers, I must ask you which of the two kinds should be rulers of our state?"[40] Well, then, "Until philosophers are kings, or the kings and princes of this world have the spirit and power of philosophy,

---

40. *Republic*, 184.

cities will never cease from ill, nor the human race."[41]
That, of course, is the heart and soul of Plato.

Dishonest Democracy

Let us get back to the circumference and approach this same point by another route.

I grant you, says Plato, that to have rulers at all is very disagreeable. And indeed we should not need to have them were it not for a regrettable but real porcine element in us. My own Utopia is not an aristocracy nor a democracy, nor any kind of an *'ocracy*; it is what some of you would call an anarchist communism. I have described it very clearly in the second book of my *Republic*, but nobody cares to notice it, except to repeat my brother's gibe about it.[42] But instead of this Utopia of mine being a "City of Pigs," it is just because we are pigs that I had to give up painting this picture and turn to describing "not only a state, but a luxurious state." I am still "of opinion that the true state, which may be said to be a healthy constitution, is the one which I have described," and not the "inflamed constitution" to which I devoted the rest of my book, and which in my opinion is much more a "City of Pigs" than the other. It is because people want "to lie on sofas, and dine off tables, and have dainties and dessert in the modern fashion, and perfumes, and incense, and courtesans, and cakes, and gold, and ivory, hunters and actors, musicians, players, dancers, tutors, servants, nurses wet and dry, barbers, confectioners and cooks, and hosts of animals (if people are to eat animals), and physicians; then a slice of neighbor's land, and then war,"[43] - in short, it is because people are pigs that you must have soldiers and rulers and laws.

But if you must have them, why not train your best men for the work, just as you train some to be doctors, and others to be lawyers, and others to be engineers? Think of taking a man's pills just because he can show a count of noses in his favor! Think of letting a man build the world's

---

41. *Ibid.*, 473.
42. The passage, abbreviated, follows: "First, then, let us consider what will be their way of life, now that we have thus established them. Will they not produce corn, and wine, and clothes, and shoes, and build houses for themselves? And when they are housed, they will work in summer commonly stripped and barefoot, but in winter substantially clothed and shod. They will feed on barley and wheat, baking the wheat and kneading the flour, making noble puddings and loaves; these they will serve up on a mat of reeds or clean leaves, themselves reclining the while upon beds of yew or myrtle boughs. And they and their children will feast, drinking of the wine which they have made, wearing garlands on their heads, and having the praises of the gods on their lips, living in sweet society, and having a care that their families do not exceed their means; for they will have an eye to poverty or war. Of course they will have a relish, salt, and olives, and cheese, and onions, and cabbages or other country herbs which are fit for boiling; and we shall give them a dessert of figs, and pulse, and beans, and myrtle berries, and beech-nuts, which they will roast at the fire, drinking in moderation. And with such a diet they may be expected to live in peace to a good old age, and bequeath a similar life to their children after them." - *Republic*, 372. Cf. The Rousseauian anthropology of *Laws*, 679.
43. *Republic*, 372-3.

greatest bridge because he is popular! You accuse me of plagiarizing from Pythagoras, but in truth, you who believe in democracy are the Pythagoreans of politics - you believe in number as your god. Your equality is the equality of the unequal, and is all a matter of words and never of reality; your liberty is anarchy, it is the congenital sickness wherein your democracy was conceived and delivered, and whereof it inevitably dies; your freedom of speech is a license to lie; your elections are a contest in flattery and prevarication. Your democracy is a theatrocracy; and woe to the genius who falls into your hands.

Perhaps you like democracy because you are like democracy: all your desires are on a level; that you should respect some of them and discipline others is an idea that never enters your heads. It has never occurred to you that it takes more time and training to make a statesman than it does to make a bootblack. But statesmanship is something that can never be conferred by plebiscite; it must be pursued through the years, and must find the privilege of office without submitting to a vote. Wisdom is too subtle a thing to be felt by the coarsened senses of the mob. Your industry is wonderful because it is shot through with specialization and training, but because you reject specialization and training in filling the offices of your government, the word politics has become dishonored in your mouths. And just because you will let anyone be your leader, no real man ever submits himself to your choice.

Culture and Slavery

There is much exaggeration here, of course, as might be expected of one whose material and social concerns were bound up with the oligarchical party at Athens, whose friends and relatives had died in battle against the armies of the democracy; whose early years had seen the democratic mismanagement of the Peloponnesian war and the growth of a disorderly individualism in Athens. But there are also lessons here for those who are strong enough to learn even from their enemies.[44] To press home these lessons at this point would take us too far afield; our plan for the moment is to follow Plato's guidance until he has led us out into a clear view of his position.

We shall suppose such a scheme of education as Plato desires; we shall suppose that a moderate number of those who entered the lists at birth have survived test after test, have "tasted the dear delight" of philosophy for five years, and have passed safely through the ordeal of practical affairs; these men (and women, as we shall see) now automatically

44. Much of modern criticism of democracy finds its inspiration in Plato. Cf. Bernard Shaw: "The democratic politician remains exactly as Plato described him." Cf. also the *Modern Utopia and Research Magnificent* of H. G. Wells. Nietzsche's debt to Plato will appear in a later chapter.

become the rulers of the Platonic state: let us observe them in their work and in their lives.

To the guardians it is a matter of first principles that the function of the state - and therefore their function - is a positive function; they are to lead the people, and not merely to serve as an umpire of disputes. They are the protagonists of a social evolution that has at last become conscious; they are resolved that henceforth social organization shall be a far-seeing plan and not a haphazard flux of expediencies of control. They know that they are asked to be experts in foresight and coordination; they will legislate accordingly, and will no more think of asking the people what laws should be passed than a physician would ask the people what measures should be taken to preserve the public health.

And first of all they will control population; they will consider this to be the indispensable prerequisite to a planned development. The state must not be larger than is consistent with unity and with the efficacy of central control. People may mate as they will - that is their own concern - but they must understand quite clearly that procreation is an affair of the state. Children must be born not of love but of science; marriage will be a temporary relation, allowing frequent remating for the sake of beautiful offspring. Men shall not have children before thirty, nor after forty. Deformed or incurably diseased children will be exposed to die. Children must leave their mothers at birth, and be brought up by the state. Women must be freed from bondage to their children, if women are to be real citizens, interested in the public weal, and loving not a narrow family but the great community.

For women are to be citizens; it would be foolish to let half the people be withdrawn from interest in and service to the state. Women will receive all the educational advantages offered to men; they will even wrestle with them, naked, in the games. If any of them - and surely some of them will - pass all the tests, they shall be guardians, too. People are to be divided, for political purposes, not by difference of sex, but by difference of capacity. Some women may be fit not for housekeeping but for ruling - let them rule; some men may be fit not for ruling but for housekeeping - let them keep house.

Without family, and without clearly ascertainable relationship between any man and any child, there can be no individual inheritance of property; the guardians will have all things in common, and without Tertullian's exception.[45] Shut off from the possibility of personal bequests or of "founding a family," the guardians will have no stimulus to laying up a hoard of material goods; nay, they will not be moved to such hoarding by fear of the morrow, for a modest but sufficient maintenance will be supplied them by the working classes. There will be no money in use among

---

45. "Omnia communia inter nos habemus, praeter mulieres."

them; they will live a hard simple life, devoted to the problems of communal defense and development. Freed from family ties, from private property and luxury, from violence and litigation, and all distinctions of Mine and Thine, they will have no reason to oppress the workers in order to lay up stores for themselves; they will be happy in the exercise of their high responsibilities and powers. They will not be tempted to legislate for the good of their own class rather than for the good of the community; their joy will lie in the creation of a prosperous and harmonious state.

Under their direction will be the soldiers, also specially selected and trained, and supported by the workers. But these workers?

They will be those who have been eliminated in the tests. The demands of specialization will have condemned them to labor for those who have the gift of guidance. They shall have no voice in the direction of the state; that, as said, is a reward for demonstrated capacity, and not a "natural right."[46] Frankly, there are some people who are not fit to be other than slaves; and to varnish that fact with oratory about "the dignity of labor" is merely to give an instance of the indignities to which a democratic politician will descend. These workers are incapable of a subtler happiness than that of knowing that they are doing what they are fit to do, and are contributing to the maintenance of communal prosperity. Such as they are, these workers, like the other members of the state, will find their highest possibilities of development in such an organized society. And to make sure that they will not rebel, they will have been taught by "royal lies" that their position and function in the state have been ordained by the gods. There is no sense in shivering at this quite judicious juggling with the facts; there are times when truth is a barrier to content, and must be set aside. Physicians have been known to cure ailments with a timely lie. Labor stimulated by such deception may be slavery, if you wish to call it so; but it is the inevitable condition of order, and order is the inevitable condition of culture and communal success.

Plasticity and Order

But is it just? - someone asks. Perhaps there are other things than order to be considered. Perhaps this hunger for order is a disease, like the monistic hunger for unity; perhaps it is a corollary to the a priori type of mind; perhaps it is part of the philosopher's general inability to face a possibly irrational reality. Here for order's sake the greater part of the people must work in silence: they shall not utter their desires. Here for order's sake are sacrificed that communal plasticity, that freedom of variety, that happy looseness and changeability of structure, in which lie all the sug-

---

46. Let us remember that a property-qualification for the vote remained in our own political system till the time of Jefferson, and has in our own day been resuscitated in some of the Southern states.

gestion and potency of social reconstruction. If there is any lesson which shines out through all the kaleidoscope of history, it is that a political system is doomed to early death if its charter offer no provision and facility for its own reform. Plasticity is king. Human ideals change, and leave nations, institutions, even gods, in their wake. "Law and order in a state are" *not* "the cause of every good";[47] they are the security of goods attained, but they may be also the hindrance of goods conceived. A state without freedom of criticism and variation is like a sailboat in a calm; it stands but it cannot move. Such a state is a geometrical diagram, a perfect syllogism evolved out of impossible premises; and its own perfection is its refutation. In such a state there could be no Plato, with a penchant for conceiving utopias; much less a Socrates, holding that a life uncriticized is unworthy of a man. It would be a state not for philosophers but for priests: very truly its basis would not be dialectical clarity but royal lies. Here is the supreme pessimism, the ultimate atheism, of the aristocrat, that he does not believe in the final wholesomeness of truth. And surely something can be said for democracy. Granted that democracy is not a problem solved but a problem added; it is at least a problem that time may help to clarify. Granted that men used to slavery cannot turn and wisely rule themselves; what is better than that they should, by inevitable trial and error, learn? *Errando discimus.* Granted that physicians do not consult us in their prescriptions; but neither do they come to us before they are chosen and called. "That the guardian should require another guardian to guard him is ridiculous indeed."[48] But he would! Power corrupts unless it is shared by all. "Cities cannot exist, if a few only share in the virtues, as in the arts "[49] To build your culture on the backs of slaves is to found your city on Vesuvius. Men will not be lied to forever - at least with the same lies! And to end with such a Utopia - what is it but to yield to Thrasymachus, to arrange all things at last in the interest of the stronger? Is it just?

The Meaning of Justice

But what is justice? asks Plato. Don't you see that our notion of justice is the very crux of the whole business? Is justice merely a matter of telling the truth? Nonsense; it may be well to have our children believe that; but those who are not children know that if a lie is a better instrument of achievement than the truth in some given juncture of events, then a lie is justified. Truth is a social value, and has its justification only in that; if untruth prove here and there of social value, then untruth is just.[50] The

---

47. *Laws*, 783.
48. *Republic*, 403.
49. *Protagoras*, 322
50. Plato, says Cleanthee, "cursed as impious him who first sundered the just from the useful,"

confusion of justice with some absolute eternal law comes of a separa-
tion of ethics from politics, and an attempt to arrive at a definition of justice from the study of individuals. But morals grow out of politics; justice
is essentially a political relation. And taking the state as a whole, it is clear
that nothing is "good" unless it works; that it would be absurd to say that
justice demands of a state that it should be ordered in such a way as to
make for its own decay. Social organization must be effective; and lies
and class-divisions are justified if they make for the effectiveness of a
political order. Surely social effectiveness forbids that men fit to legislate
should live out their lives as cobblers, or that men should rule whose natural aptitude is for digging ditches. Justice means, for politics at least, that
each member of society is minding his natural business, is doing that for
which he is fitted by his own natural capacity. Injustice is the encroach-
ment of one part on another; justice is the efficient functioning of each
part. Justice, then, is social coordination and harmony. It is not "the interest of the stronger," it is the harmony of the whole. So in the individual,
justice is the harmonious operation of a unified personality; each element
in one's nature doing that which it is fitted to do; again it is not mere
strength or forcefulness, but harmonious, organized strength; it is effective order. And effective order demands a class division. You may mouth
as you please the delusive delicacies of democracy; but classes you will
have, for men will always be some of gold and some of silver and some
of brass. And the brass must not pass itself off as silver, nor the silver as
gold. Give the brass all the time and opportunity in the world, and it will
still be brass. Of course brass will not believe that it is brass, but we had
better make it understand once for all that it is so, even if we have to tell
a thousand lies to get the truth believed.

And as for variation and plasticity, remember that these too are val-
ueless except as they make for a better society. They assuredly make for
change; but change is not betterment. History is a chaos of variations;
without some organ for their control they cancel one another and termi-
nate inevitably in futility. Our problem is not how to change, but how to set
our best brains to controlling change for the sake of a finer life.

The Future of Plato

There are *apercus* here, and a bewildering wealth of suggestions,
which one is tempted to pursue to their ultimate present significance. But
to do that would be to encroach too much on the subjects of later chapters. The vital thing here is not to accept or refute any special element in
Plato's political philosophy; it is rather to see how inextricably politics and
philosophy were bound together in his mind as two sides of fundamen-

---

- Gomperz, II, 73. Cf. *Republic*, 331.

tally one endeavor. Here is the passion to remold things; here is the seeing of perfection and the will to make perfection; here speaks out for the
first time in European history the courage of the intellect that not only will
perceive but will remake. Here is a man; no dead academic cobweb-
weaver, but a masterful, kingly soul, mixed up in warm intimacy with the
complex flow of the life about him. He paints Utopia; but at the same time
he takes his own counsel anent the importance of an educational
approach to the social problem, and founds the most famous and influential university the world has ever seen. Picture him in the gardens and
lecture-halls of his Academy, arranging and supervising and coordinating,
and turning out men to whom nations looked - and not in vain - for statesmen. Not merely to lift men up to the beatific vision of unities and perfec-
tions, but to teach them the art of creation, to fire them with the ardor of
a new artistry; this he aimed to do, and did. "The greatest works grow in
importance, as trees do after the death of the mortal men who planted
them." So grew the Republic, and the Academy.[51]

To catch in a chapter the deep yet subtle spirit and meaning of this
"finest product of antiquity,"[52] - it is not easy. In Plato's Utopia there would
no doubt have been a law against writing so briefly on so vast a phenomenon, with, in this case, the inevitably consequent derangement of
the Platonic perspective, and the impossibility, within such compass, of
focusing Plato in the political and philosophical meaning of his time.
One's feeling here is of having desecrated with small talk the Parthenon
of philosophy. Perhaps as we go on we shall be able to see more clearly
the still-living value of Plato's thought: in almost everything that we shall
hereinafter discuss his voice will be heard, even though unnamed. Today,
at last, he comes again into his own - as in Renaissance days - after centuries dominated by the influence of his first misinterpreter; and generations bred on the throned lukewarmness of the *Nicomachean Ethics* yield
to a generation that is learning to feel the hot constructive passion of the
Republic. Dead these two thousand and some hundred years, Plato
belongs to the future.

51. Edmund Gosse, *Life of Henrik Ibsen*, p, 100.
52. Nietzsche, *Beyond Good and Evil*, pref.

CHAPTER THREE
FRANCIS BACON AND
THE SOCIAL POSSIBILITIES OF SCIENCE

From Plato to Bacon

"As I read Plato," writes Professor Dewey,[53] "philosophy began with some sense of its essentially political basis and mission - a recognition that its problems were those of the organization of a just social order. But it soon got lost in dreams of another world."[54] Plato and Aristotle are the *crura cerebri* of Europe. But in Aristotle, along with a wealth of acute observation of men and institutions, we find a diminishing interest in reconstruction; the Stagirite spent too much of his time in card-cataloguing Plato, and allowed his imagination to become suffocated with logic. With the Stoics and Epicureans begin that alienation of ethics from politics, and that subordination of philosophy to religious needs, which it is part of the task of present thinking to undo. Alexander had conquered the Orient, only to have Orientalism conquer Greece. Under Scholasticism it was the fate of great minds to retrace worn paths in the cage of a system of conclusions determined by external authority; and the obligation to uphold the established precluded any practical recognition of the reconstructive function of thought. With the Renaissance - that Indian summer of Greek culture - the dream of a remolded world found voice again. Campanella, through the darkness of his prison cell, achieved the vision of a communist utopia; and other students of the rediscovered Plato painted similar pictures. Indeed this reawakening of Plato's influence gave to the men of the Renaissance an inspiriting sense of the wonders that lay potential in organized intelligence. Again men faced the task of replacing with a natural ethic the falling authoritarian sanctions of supernatural religion; and for a time one might have hoped that the thought of Socrates was to find at last its due fruition. But again men lost themselves in the notion of a cultured class moving leisurely over the backs of slaves; and perhaps it was well that the whole movement was halted by the more Puritan but also more democratic outburst of the Reformation. What the world needed was a method which offered hope for the redemption not of

---

53. John Dewey, another of Will Durant's professors at Colombia University. Dewey was a pioneer in twentieth century philosophy and psychology and one of the founders of the philosophical school of thought known as *Pragmatism*.
54. *Influence of Darwin on Philosophy*, New York, 1910, p.21.

a class, but of all. Galileo and Roger Bacon opened the way to meeting this need by their emphasis on the value of hypothesis and experiment, and the necessity of combining induction with deduction; it remained for Francis Bacon to layout the road for the organized employment of these new methods, and to inspire all Europe with his warm vision of their social possibilities.

Character

If you would understand Bacon, you must see him as not so much a philosopher as an administrator. You find him a man of great practical ability: he remolds philosophy with one hand and rules part of England with the other; not to speak of writing Shakespeare's plays between times! He rises brilliantly from youthful penury to the political pinnacle; and meanwhile he runs over the whole realm of human knowledge, scattering praise and censure with lordly hand. Did we not know the fact as part of the history of England we should never suspect that the detailed and varied learning of this man was the incidental accomplishment of a life busied with political intrigue. *Bene vixit qui bene latuit*: surely here is a man who has lived widely, and in no merely physical sense has made the world his home. Life is no "brief candle" to him, nor men "such stuff as dreams are made of"; life is a glorious gift, big with blessing for him who will but assist at the delivery. There is nothing of the timid ascetic about him; like Socrates, he knows that there is a sort of cowardice in shunning pleasure;[55] best of all, there is so much work to be done, so many opportunities for the man of unnarrowed soul. He feels the exhilaration of one who has burst free from the shackles of intellectual authority: he sees before him an uncharted future, raw material for hands that dare to mold it; and he dares: All his life long he is mixed up with the heart of things; every day is an adventure. Exiled from politics, he plunges gladly into the field of scientific reconstruction; he does not forget that he is an administrator, any more than Plato could forget that he was a dramatist; he finds the world of thought a chaos, and bequeaths it a planful process for the coordination of human life; all Europe responds to his call for the "enlarging of the bounds of human empire." He works joyfully and buoyantly to the very last, and dies as he has wished, "in an earnest pursuit, which is like one that is wounded in hot blood, who, for the time, scarce feels the hurt."

The Expurgation of the Intellect

Consider the reaction of an experienced statesman who leaves the

---

55. Cf. *De Augmentis*, bk. VIII, Ch. 2.

service of a king to enter the service of truth. He has left a field wherein all workers moved in subordination to one head and one focal purpose; he enters a field in which each worker is working by himself, with no division of labor, no organization of endeavor, no correlation of ends. There he has found administration, here he finds a naive *laissez-faire*; there order, here anarchy; there some sense of common end and effort, here none. He understands at once the low repute of philosophy among men of affairs. "For the people are very apt to contemn truth, upon account of the controversies raised about it; and so think those all in a wrong way, who never meet."[56] He understands at once why it is that the world has been so little changed by speculation and research. He is a man whose consciousness of pervasive human misery is too sharp for comfort;[57] and he sees no hope of remedy for this in isolated guerilla attacks waged upon the merest outposts of truth, each attack with its jealously peculiar strategy, its own dislocated, almost irrelevant end. And yet if there is no remedy for men's ills in this nascent science and renascent philosophy, in what other quarter, then, shall men look for hope and cure?

There is no other, Bacon feels; unless victory is first won in the laboratory and the study it will never be won in political assemblies; no plebiscite or royal edict, but only truth, can make men free. Man's hope lies in the reorganization of the processes of discovery and interpretation. Unless philosophy and science be born again of social aims and social needs they cannot have life in them. A new spirit must enter.

But first old spirits must be exorcised. Speculation and research must bring out a declaration of independence against theology. "The corruption of philosophy by superstition and an admixture of theology is widely spread, and does the greatest harm."[58] The search for final causes, for design in nature, must be left to theologians; the function of science is not to interpret the purposes of nature, but to discover the connections of cause and effect in nature. Dogma must be set aside: "if a man will begin with certainties he shall end in doubts; but if he will be content to begin in doubts he shall end in certainties."[59] Dogma must be set aside, too, because it necessitates deduction as a basic method; and deduction as a basic method is disastrous.

But that is not all; there is much more in the way of preliminaries: there must be a general "expurgation of the intellect." The mind is full (some would say made up) of prejudices, wild fancies, "idols," or imaginings of things that are not so: if you are to think correctly, usefully, all these must go. Try, then, to get as little of yourself as possible in the way of the thing you wish to see. Beware of the very general tendency to put

56. *Advancement of Learning*, Boston, 1863, bk. I.
57. *Philosophical Works*, ed, J. M. Robertson, London, 1806, p. 33.
58. *Novum Organum.* i. 65.
59. *Advancement of Learning*, p. 133.

order and regularity in the world and then to suppose that they are native to the structure of things; or to force all facts into the unyielding mold of a preconceived opinion, carefully neglecting all contrary instances; or to give too credulous an ear to that which flatters the wish. Look into yourself and see the forest of prejudices that has grown up within you: through your temperamental attitudes; through your education; through your friends (friendship is so often an agreement in prejudices); through your favorite authors and authorities. If you find yourself seizing and dwelling on anything with particular satisfaction, hold it in suspicion. Beware of words, for they are imposed according to the apprehension of the crowd; make sure that you do not take abstractions for things. And remind yourself occasionally that you are not the measure of all things, but their distorting mirror.

So much by way of clearing the forest. Comes then induction as the fount and origin of all truth: patient induction, obedient to the call of fact, and with watchful eye for, above all things, the little unwelcome instance that contradicts. Not that induction is everything; it includes experiment, of course, and is punctuated by hypothesis.[60] (More, it is clearly but the servant of deduction, since the aim of all science is to predict by deduction from generalizations formed by induction; but just as clear is it that the efficacy of the whole business lies grounded in the faithfulness of the induction: induction is servant, but it has all men at its mercy.) And to formulate methods of induction, to surround the process by mechanical guards, to protect it from the premature flights of young generalizations - that is a matter of life and death to science.

Knowledge is Power

And now, armed with these methods of procedure, we stand face to face with nature. What shall we ask her? *Prudens questio dimidium scientiae*: to know what to ask is half of every science.

You must ask for laws or, to use a Platonic term, forms. In every process there is matter and there is form: the matter being the seat of the process or operation, and the form its method or law. "Though in nature nothing really exists besides individual bodies, performing pure individual acts, according to a fixed law, yet in philosophy the very law, and the investigation, discovery, and explanation of it, is the foundation as well of knowledge as of operation. And it is this law; with its clauses, that I mean when I speak of Forms."[61] Not so much what a "thing" is, but how it behaves - that is the question. And what is more, if you will examine your conception of a "thing," you will see that it is really a conception of how

---

60. Called by Bacon the "first vintage."
61. *Novum Organum*, II, 2.

the "thing" behaves; every *What* is at last a *How*. Every "thing" is a machine, whose essence or meaning is to be found not by a mere description of its parts, but by an account of how it operates. "How does it work?" asks the boy before a machine; see to it that you ask the same question of nature.

For observe, if you know how a thing works, you are on the way to managing and controlling it. Indeed, a Form can be defined as those elements in a process which must be known before the process can be controlled. Here we see the meaning of science; it is an effort to discover the laws which must be known in order "that the mind may exercise her power over the nature of things."[62] Science is the formulation of control; knowledge is power. The object of science is not merely to know, but to rebuild; every science longs to be an art. The quest for knowledge, then, is not a matter of curiosity; it is a fight for power. We "put nature on the rack and compel her to bear witness" against herself. Where this conception reigns, logic-chopping is out of court. "The end of our new logic is to find not arguments but arts, not probable reasons but plans and designs of works, to overcome not an adversary in argument but nature in action."[63]

But there is logic-chopping in other things than logic. All strife of men with men, of group with group, if it leaves no result beyond the victory and passing supremacy of the individual or group, is logic-chopping. Such victories pass from side to side, and cancel themselves into final nullity. Real achievement is victory, not over other men but with them. "It will not be amiss to distinguish the three kinds, and as it were grades, of ambition in mankind. The first is of those who desire to extend their own power in their native country, which kind is vulgar and degenerate. The second is of those who labor to extend the power of their country and its dominion among men. This certainly has more dignity, though not less covetousness. But if a man endeavor to establish and extend the power and dominion of the human race over the universe, his ambition is without doubt both a more wholesome thing and a more noble than the other two. The empire of man over things depends wholly on the arts and sciences. For we cannot command nature except by obeying her."[64]

The Socialization of Science

Natura non vincitur nisi parendo. "I accept the universe," says Margaret Fuller. "Gad! You'd better!" says Carlyle. "I accept it," says Bacon, "but only as raw material. We will listen to nature, but only that we

---

62. Preface to *Magna Instauratio*.
63. *Novum Organum*, pref.
64. *Novum Organum*, I, 129.

may learn what language she understands. We stoop to conquer."

There is nothing impossible but thinking makes it so. "By far the greatest obstacle to the progress of science and the undertaking of new tasks . . . is found in this, that men despair and think things impossible. If therefore any one believes or promises more, they think this comes of an ungoverned and unripened mind."[65] There is nothing that we may not do, if we *will*, but we must will, and must will the means as well as the end. Would we have an empire of man over nature? Very well: organize the arts and sciences.

"Consider what may be expected from men abounding in leisure, and from association of labors, and from successions of ages; the rather because it is not a way over which only one man can pass at a time (as is the case with that of reasoning), but within which the labors and industries of men (especially as regards the collecting of experience) may with the best effort be distributed and then combined. For then only will men begin to know their strength when instead of great numbers doing all the same things, one shall take charge of one thing and another of another."[66] There should be more cooperation, less chaotic rivalry, in research. And the cooperation should be international; the various universities of the world, so far as they engage in research, should be like the different buildings of a great manufacturing plant, each with its own particular specialty and quest. Is it not remarkable how "little sympathy and correspondence exists between colleges and universities, as well throughout Europe as in the same state and kingdom?"[67] Why cannot all the research in the world be coordinated into one unified advance? Perhaps the truth-seekers would be unwilling, but has that been shown? And is the number of willing cooperators too small to warrant further effort? How can we know without the trial? Grant that the genius would balk at some external central direction; but research after all is seldom a matter of genius. "The course I propose . . . is such as leaves but little to the acuteness and strength of wits, but places all wits and understandings nearly on the level."[68] Let scope and freedom be amply provided for the genius; it is the work of following up the *apercus* of genius that most sorely needs coordination. Organization of research means really the liberation of genius: liberation from the halting necessities of mechanical repetition in experiment. Nor is coordination regimentation; let each man follow his hobby to whatever university has been assigned to the investigation of that particular item. Liberty is futility unless it is organized.

It is a plan, you see, for the socialization of science. It is a large and royal vision; to make it real involves "indeed *opera basilica*," it is the busi-

---

65. *Ibid.*, 92.
66. *Ibid.*, 113.
67. *Advancement of Learning*, bk. II, ch. 1.
68. *Novum Organum*, I, 61.

ness of a king, "towards which the endeavors of one man can be but as the sign on a crossroad, which points out the way but cannot tread it."[69] It will need such legislative appropriations as are now granted only to the business of competitive destruction on land and sea. "As the secretaries and spies of princes and states bring in bills for intelligence, so you must allow the spies and intelligencers of nature to bring in their bills if you would not be ignorant of many things worthy to be known. And if Alexander placed so large a treasure at Aristotle's command for the support of hunters, fowlers, fishers and the like, in much more need do they stand of this beneficence who unfold the labyrinths of nature."[70]

Science and Utopia

Such an organization of science is Bacon's notion of Utopia. He gives us in *The New Atlantis*, in plain strong prose, a picture of a state in which this organization has reached the national stage. It is a state nominally ruled by a king (Bacon never forgets that he is a loyal subject and counselor of James I); but "preeminent amongst the excellent acts of the king . . . was the erection and institution of an Order or Society which we call Solomon's House; the noblest foundation, as we think, that ever was upon the earth, and the lantern of this kingdom. It is dedicated to the study of the nature of all things."[71] Every twelve years this Order sends out to all parts of the world "merchants of light"; men who remain abroad for twelve years, gather information and suggestions in every field of art and science, and then (the next expedition having brought men to replace them) return home laden with books, instruments, inventions, and ideas. "Thus, you see, we maintain a trade not for gold, silver or jewels; nor for silk; nor for spices; nor for any other commodity or matter; but only for God's first creation, which was Light."[72] Meanwhile at home there is a busy army filling many laboratories, experimenting in zoology, medicine, dietetics, chemistry, botany, physics, and other fields; there are, in addition to these men, "three that collect the experiments in all the books, three that try new experiments," three that tabulate the results of the experimenters; "three that look into the experiments of their fellows, and cast about how to draw out of them things of use . . . for man's life; . . . three that direct new experiments"; three that from the results draw up "observations, axioms, and aphorisms."[73] "We imitate also the flights of birds; we have some degree of flying in the air; we have ships and boats for going under water."[74] And the purpose of it all, he says, with fine

---

69. *Advancement of Learning*, bk. I, ch. 1.
70. *Ibid.*, bk. II, ch. 1.
71. *New Atlantis*, Cambridge University Press, 1900, p. 22.
72. *Ibid.*, p. 24.
73. Pp. 44, 45.
74. P. 43.

Baconian ring, is "the enlarging of the bounds of human empire, to the effecting of all things possible."[75]

Scholasticism in Science

This is the voice of the Renaissance, speaking with some method to its music. It is the voice of Erasmus rather than that of Luther; but it is the voice of a larger and less class-bound vision than that which moved the polite encomiast of folly. Such minds as were not lost in the religious turmoil of the time responded to Bacon's call for a new beginning; a "sense of liberation . . . of new destinies, pulsates in that generation at Bacon's touch."[76] Bacon says, and with justice, that he "rang the bell which called the wits together."[77] When, in 1660, a group of London savants formed the Royal Society, it was from Bacon that they took their inspiration, and from the "House of Solomon" part of their plan of organization. Diderot and D' Alembert acknowledged the impetus given by their reading of Bacon to the adventurous enterprise which completed and distributed the *Encyclopédie* despite the prohibition of the king. Today, after two hundred years of Cartesian futility about mind and body and the problem of knowledge, the Baconian emphasis on the socially-reconstructive function of thought renews its power and appeal. The world returns to Socrates, to Plato, and to Bacon.

But with some measure of wholesome disillusionment. These last two centuries have told us that science, unaided, cannot solve our social problem. We have invented, invented, invented, invented; and with what result? The gap between class and class has so widened during these inventive years that there are now not classes but castes. Social harmony is a matter of brief interludes in a drama more violent than any ever mimicked on the stage. Men trained and accomplished in science, like Prince Kropotkin, abandon it on the score that it has turned its back on the purpose that gave it vitality and worth.[78]

What is the purpose of science? What do scientists consider to be the purpose of science? The laboratories are crowded with men who have no inkling of any other than a purely material reconstruction as the function of their growing knowledge. Specialization has so divided science that hardly any sense of the whole survives. The ghosts of scholasticism - of a pursuit of knowledge divorced from its social end - hover about the microscopes and test tubes of the scientific world; and the upshot of it all is that to them who have, more is given. Let Bacon speak here: "There is another great and powerful cause why the sciences have made but little

---

75. P. 34.
76. J. M. Robertson, preface to *Philosophical Works*.
77. Robert Adamson, article "Bacon," *Encyclopedia Britannica*.
78. Cf. Preface to *Memoirs of a Revolutionist*.

progress, which is this. It is not possible to run a course aright, when the goal itself has not been rightly placed."[79] Sciences with obvious social functions have languished through lapse of all sense of direction, all feeling of focus; psychology, for example, is but now reviving under the stimulus of men who dared to "stir the earth a little about the roots of this science,"[80] because they had perceived its purpose and meaning in the drama of reconstruction. The blunt truth is that unless a scientist is also a philosopher, with some capacity to see things *sub specie totius* - unless he can come out of his hole into the open, - he is not fit to direct his own research. "As no perfect discovery can be made upon a flat or level, neither is it possible to discover the more remote and deeper parts of any science, if you stand but upon the level of the same science, and ascend not to a higher science."[81] Before it can be of real service to life, science must be enlightened by some discrimination of values, some consideration and fitting together of human ends: without philosophy as its eye piece, science is but the traditional child who has taken apart the traditional watch, with none but the traditional results.

There is more to this indictment. Science has been organized, though very imperfectly, for research; it has been organized hardly at all for social application and control. The notion that science can be used in conserving the vital elements of order and at the same time facilitating experimental and progressive change, is but beginning to walk about. Indeed, the employment and direction of scientific ability in the business of government is still looked upon as a doubtful procedure; to say that the administration of municipal affairs, for example, is to be given over to men trained in the social sciences rather than to men artful in trapping votes with oratorical molasses, is still a venture into the loneliness of heresy. Again let Bacon speak, who was administrator and philosopher in one. "It is wrong to trust the natural body to empirics who commonly have a few receipts whereon they rely, but who know neither the causes of the disease, nor the constitution of patients, nor the danger of accidents, nor the true methods of cure. And so it must needs be dangerous to have the civil body of states managed by empirical statesmen, unless well mixed with others who are grounded in learning. On the contrary it is almost without instance that any government was unprosperous under learned governors."[82]

Plato over again, you say. Yes, just as "Greek philosophy is the dough with which modern philosophers have baked their bread, kneading it over and over again,"[83] so this vital doctrine of the application of the

---

79. *Novum Organum*, I, 81.
80. *Advancement of Learning*, p. 297.
81. *Ibid.*, p. 131.
82. *Advancement of Learning*, bk. I.
83. Professor Woodbridge, class lectures.

best available intelligence to the problem of social order and development must be restated in every generation until at last the world may see its truth and merit exemption from its repetition.

The Asiatics of Europe

But the place of Bacon in the continuum of history is hardly stated by connecting him with Plato. Conceive of him rather as a new protagonist in the long epic of intelligence; another blow struck in the seemingly end-less war between magic and science, between supernaturalism and nat-uralism, between the spirit of worship and the spirit of control. Primitive man - and he lives everywhere under the name of legion - looks out upon nature as something to be feared and obeyed, something to be cajoled by ritual and sacrifice and prayer. In ages of great social disorder, such as the millennium inaugurated in Western Europe by the barbarian inva-sions, the primitive elements in the mental makeup of men emerge through the falling cultural surface; and cults rich in ritual and steeped in emotional luxury grow in rank abundance. It is in the character of man to worship power: if he feels the power without him more intensely than the power within, he worships nature with a humble fear, and leans on magic and supernatural rewards; if he feels the power within him more intense-ly than the power without, he sees divinity in himself and other centers of remolding activity, and thinks not of worshipping and obeying nature, but of controlling and commanding her. The second attitude comes, of course, with knowledge, and action that expresses knowledge; it is quite human that nature should not be worshipped once she has been known. A man is primitive, then, when he worships nature and makes no effort to control her; he is mature when he stops worshipping and begins to con-trol - when he understands that "Nature is not a temple but a workshop,"[84] not a barrier to divinity, but the raw material of Utopia.

Now the essence of Bacon is not the replacement of deduction by induction, but the change of emphasis from worship to control. This emphasis, once vivid in Plato but soon obscured by Oriental influence, is one of the two dominant elements in modern thought (the other being the puzzling over an artificial problem of knowledge); and unless the Baconian element finally subordinates the Cartesian, the word modern must no longer arrogate to itself a eulogistic connotation. Hence Bacon, and not Descartes, is the initiator of modern philosophy; part initiator, at least, of that current of thought which finds rebellious expression in the enlightenment of the eighteenth century, and comes to supremacy in the scientific victories of the nineteenth. The vital sequence in modern phi-losophy is not Descartes, Berkeley, Kant, Hegel, and Bergson (for these

---

84. Turgenev, in *Fathers and Children*.

are the Asiatics of Europe), but Bacon, Hobbes, Condorcet, Comte, Darwin, and James.[85]

The hope of the world is in this resolute spirit of control - control of the material without us, and of the passions within. Bit by bit, one is not afraid to say, we shall make for ourselves a better world. Shall we not find a way to eliminate disease, to control the increase of population, to find in plastic organization a substitute for revolution? Shall we perhaps even succeed in transmuting the lust for power over man into ambition to conquer the forces that impede man? Shall we make men understand that there is more potency of joy in the sense of having contributed to the power of men over nature than in any personal triumph of one over another man? More glory in a conquest of bacteria than in all the martial victories that have ever spilled human blood? Here is the beginning of real civilization, and the mark of man. "The environment transforms the animal; man transforms the environment."[86] "Looking at the history of the world as a whole, the tendency has been in Europe to subordinate nature to man; out of Europe, to subordinate man to nature. Formerly the richest countries were those in which nature was most bountiful; now the richest countries are those in which man is most active."[87] Control is the sign of maturity, the achievement of Europe, the future of America. It is, one argues again, the drama of history, this war between Asia and Europe, between nature and man, between worship and control. Fundamentally it is the upward struggle of intelligence: Plato is its voice, Zeno its passing exhaustion, Bacon its resurrection. It was not an unopposed rebirth: there is still no telling whether East or West will win. Surrounded by the backwash of Oriental currents everywhere, the lover of the Baconian spirit needs constantly to refresh himself at the fount of Bacon's inexhaustible inspiration and confidence. "I stake all," he says, "on the victory of art over nature through the Pillars of Hercules out into the unknown sea, and over it the words, PLUS ULTRA.

More beyond!

---

85. This division into saints and sinners must be taken with reservations, of course. In many respects Descartes belongs to the second group, and in some respects James and Comte belong to the first. But the dichotomy clarifies, if only by exaggeration.
86. L. Ward, *Pure Sociology*, p. 16.
87. Buckle, *History of Civilization*, I, 138.

CHAPTER FOUR
SPINOZA ON THE SOCIAL PROBLEM [88]

Hobbes

Passing from Bacon to Spinoza we meet with Thomas Hobbes, a man from whom Spinoza drew many of his ideas, though very little of his inspiration. The social incidence of the greater part of Hobbes's thinking has long been recognized; he is not a figure over whom the biographer of social thought finds much cause to quarrel. He is at once the materialist *par excellence* of modern philosophy, and the most uncompromising protagonist of the absolutist theory of the state. The individual, all compact of pugnacity, was to Hobbes the bogey which the state, voracious of all liberties, became two centuries later to Herbert Spencer. He had in acute degree the philosopher's natural appetite for order; and trembled at the thought of initiatives not foreseen by his political geometry. He lived in the midst of alarms: war stepped on the heels of war in what was very nearly a real *bellum omnium contra omnes*. He lived in the midst of political reaction: men were weary of Renaissance exuberance and Reformation strife, and sank gladly into the open arms of the past. There could be no end, thought Hobbes, to this turmoil of conflicting egos, individual and national, until all groups and individuals knelt in absolute obedience to one sovereign power.

But all this has been said before; we need but remind ourselves of it here so that we may the better appreciate the vibrant sympathy for the individual man, the generous defense of popular liberties, that fill with the glow of subdued passion the pages of the gentle Spinoza.

The Spirit of Spinoza [89]

Yet Spinoza was not wanting in that timidity and that fear of unbridled instinct which stood dictator over the social philosophy of Hobbes. He knew as well as Hobbes the dangers of a democracy that could not dis-

88. Special acknowledgment for some of the material of this chapter is due to R. A. Duff. *Spinoza's Political and Ethical Philosophy*, Glasgow, 1903.
89. Spinoza, more than any other philosopher, had possibly the most profound philosophical effect on Will Durant. While working as a librarian at Seminary school, Durant had come across a copy of Spinoza's *Ethics*. "When I had finished the book, and then finished it again, I knew that the *Ethics* would be on of the strongest influences of my life." (Source: *Transition*, Will Durant. p. 136.) The philosophical effect Spinoza's arguments caused him to question the existence of God and would culminate in Durant's abandonment of the priesthood and his departure from the seminary.

cipline itself. "Those who have had experience of how changeful the temper of the people is, are almost in despair. For the populace is governed not by reason but by emotion; it is headlong in everything, and easily corrupted by avarice and luxury."[70] And even more than Hobbes he withdrew from the affairs of men and sought in the protection of a suburban attic the peace and solitude which were the vital medium of his thought. He found that sometimes at least, "truth hath a quiet breast." "*Se tu sarai solo*," wrote Leonardo, "*tu sarai tutto tuo*." And surely Goethe thought of Spinoza when he said: "No one can produce anything important unless he isolate himself."

But this dread of the crowd was only a part of Spinoza's nature, and not the dominant part. His fear of men was lost in his boundless capacity for affection; he tried so hard to understand men that he could not help but love them. "I have labored carefully not to mock, lament, or execrate, but to understand, human actions; and to this end I have looked upon passions ... not as vices of human nature, but as properties just as pertinent to it as are heat, cold, storm, thunder, and the like to the nature of the atmosphere."[91] Even the accidents of time and space were sinless to his view, and all the world found room in the abundance of his heart. "Spinoza deified the All in order to find peace in the face of it," says Nietzsche:[92] but perhaps, too, because all love is deification.

All in all, history shows no man more honest and independent; and the history of philosophy shows no man so sincere, so far above quibbling and dispute and the picking of petty flaws, so eager to receive the truth even when brought by the enemy, so ready to forgive even persecution in the depth and breadth of his tolerance. No man who suffered so much injustice made so few complaints. He became great because he could merge his own suffering in the suffering of all - a mark of all deep men. "They who have not suffered," says Ibsen, and, one might add, suffered with those they saw suffer, "never create; they only write books."

Spinoza did not write much; the long-suffering are seldom long-winded. A fragment *On the Improvement of the Understanding*; a brief volume on religion and the state; the *Ethics*; and as he began to write the chapter on democracy in the *Political Treatise* consumption conquered him. Bacteria take no bribes.

Political Ethics

Had he lived longer it would have dawned perhaps even on the German historians that Spinoza's basic interest was not in metaphysics

90. *Tractatus Theologico-Politicus*, ch. 17.
91. *Tractatus Theologico-Politicus*, ch. 1.
92. *Will to Power*, vol. I, p. 96.

so much as in political ethics. The *Ethics*, because it is the most sustained flight of reasoning in philosophy, has gathered round it all the associations that throng about the name of Spinoza, so that one is apt to think of him in terms of a mystical "pantheism" rather than of coordinative intelligence, democracy, and free thought.[93] Hoffding considers it a defect in Spinoza's philosophy that it takes so little notice of epistemology: but should we not be grateful for that? Here are men suffering, said Spinoza, here are men enslaved by passions and prelates and kings; surely till these things are dealt with we have no time for epistemological delicacies. Instead of increasing the world's store of learned ignorance by writing tomes on the possibility of a subject knowing an object, Spinoza thought it better to give himself to the task of helping to keep alive in an age of tyrannical reaction the Renaissance doctrine of popular sovereignty. Instead of puzzling himself and others about epistemology, he pondered the problem of stimulating the growth of intelligence and evolving a rational ethic. He thought that philosophy was something more than a chess-game for professors.

There is no need to spend time and space here on what for Spinoza, as for Socrates and Plato, was the problem of problems, - how human reason could be developed to a point where it might replace supernatural sanctions for social conduct and provide the medium of social reconstruction. One point, however, may be profitably emphasized.

A careless reading of the *Ethics* may lead to the belief that Spinoza bases his philosophy on a naive opposition of reason to passion. It is not so. "A desire cannot be restrained or removed," says Spinoza, "except by an opposite and stronger desire "[94] Reason is not dictator to desire, it is a relation among desires, - that relation which arises when experience has hammered impulses into coordination. An impulse, passion or emotion is by itself' a confused idea," a blurred picture of the thing that is indeed desired. Thought and impulse are not two kinds of mental process: thought is impulse clarified by experience, impulse is thought in chaos.

Is Man a Political Animal?

Why is there a social problem? Is it because men are "bad"? Nonsense, answers Spinoza: the terms "good" and "bad," as conveying moral approval and disapproval, are philosophically out of court; they

93. Cf. Duff, *op. cit.*, pref.: "It can be shown that Spinoza had no interest in metaphysics for its own sake, while he was passionately interested in moral and political problems. He was a metaphysician at all only in the sense that he was resolute in thinking out the ideas, principles, and categories which are interwoven with all our practical endeavor, and the proper understanding of which is the condition of human welfare."
94. *Ethics*, bk, IV, prop. 7.

mean nothing except that "each of us wishes all men to live according to his desire," and consoles himself for their non-complaisance by making moral phrases. There is a social problem, says Spinoza, because men are not naturally social. This does not mean that there are no social tendencies in the native human constitution; it does mean that these tendencies are but a sorry fraction of man's original nature, and do not avail to chain the "ape and tiger" hiding under his extremely civilized shirt. Man is a "political animal", but he is also an animal. We must approach the social problem through a very respectful consideration of the ape and tiger, we must follow Hobbes and inquire into "the natural condition of man."

"In the state of nature every man lives as he wishes,"[95] he is not pestered with police regulations and aldermanic ordinances. He "may do whatever he can: his rights extend to the utmost limits of his powers."[96] He may fight, hate, deceive, exploit, to his heart's desire; and he does. We moderns smile at the "natural man" as a myth, and think our forbears were social *ab initio.* But be it remembered that by "social" Spinoza implies no mere preference of society to solitude, but a subordination of individual caprice to more or less tacit communal regulation. And Spinoza considers it useful, if we are going to talk about "human nature in politics", to ask whether man *naturally* submits to regulation or naturally rebels against it. When he wrote of a primitive non-social human condition, he wrote as a psychologist inferring the past rather than as an historian revealing it. He observed man, kindly yet keenly; he saw that "everyone desires to keep down his fellow men by all possible means, and when he prevails, boasts more of the injuries he has done to others than of the advantage he has won for himself",[97] and he concluded that if we could trace human history to its sources we should find a creature - call him human or pre-human willing, perhaps glad, to have the company of his like, but still unattracted and unhampered by social organization.

We like to laugh at the simple anthropology of Spinoza and Rousseau; but the laugh should be turned upon us when we suppose that the historical *motif* played any but a very minor part in the discussion of the natural state of man. History was not the point at all: these men were not interested in the past so much as in the possibilities of the future. That is why the eighteenth century was so largely their creation. When a man is interested in the past he writes history; when he is interested in the future he makes it.

The point to be borne in mind, Spinoza urges, is that we are still essentially unsocialized; the instinct to acquire possession and power, if

---

95. *Tractatus Theologico-Politicus,* V, 2.
96. *Ibid.*, ch. 16.
97. *Ethics,* bk. IV, prop. 58.

necessary by oppression and exploitation, is still stronger than the disposition to share, to be tolerant of disagreement, and to work in mutual aid. The "natural man" is not a myth, he is the solid reality that struts about dressed in a little brief civilization. "Religion teaches that each man should love his neighbor as himself, and defend the rights of others as earnestly as he would his own. Yet this conviction has very little influence over man's emotions. It is no doubt of some account in the hour of death, for then disease has weakened the emotions, and the man lies helpless. And the principle is assented to in church, for there men have no dealings with one another. But in the mart or the court it has little or no effect, though that is just where the need for it is greatest."[98] He still "does everything for the sake of his own profit";[99] nor will even the unlimited future change him in that, for it is his very essence. His happiness is in the pursuit of his profit, his supreme joy is in the increase of his power. And a social order built upon any other basis than this exuberant egoism of man will be as lasting, in the eye of history, as a name that is writ in water.

What the Social Problem Is

But what if it is a good basis? What if "the foundation of virtue is the endeavor to preserve one's own being" to the uttermost?[100] What if there is a way in which, without any hypocritical mystification, this self-seeking, while still remaining self-seeking, may become cooperation?

Spinoza's answer is not startling: it is the Socratic answer, issuing from a profound psychological analysis. Given the liberation and development of intelligence, and the discordant strife of egos will yield undreamed-of harmonies. Men are so made, they are so compact of passion and obscurity, that they will not let one another be free; how can that be changed? Deception has been tried, and has succeeded only temporarily if at all. Compulsion has been tried; but compulsion is a negative force, it makes for inhibition rather than inspiration. It is a necessary evil, but hardly the last word of constructive social thinking. There is something more in a man than his capacity for fear, there is some other way of appealing to him than the way of threats; there is his hunger and thirst to know and understand and develop. Think of the untouched resources of this human desire for mental enlargement; think of the millions who almost starve that they may learn. Is that the force that is to build the future and fashion the city of our dreams? Here are men torn with impulses, shaken by mutual interference; is it conceivable that they would be so deeply torn and shaken if that hunger of theirs for knowledge - knowledge

---

98. *Tractatus Theologico-Politicus*, I, 5.
99. *Ethics*, bk. I, appendix.
100. *Ibid.*, IV, prop. 18.

of themselves, too - were met with generous opportunity? Men long to be reasonable; they know, even the least of them, that under the tyranny of impulse there is no ultimately fruitful life; what is there that they would not give for the power to see things clearly and be captains of their souls? Here if anywhere is an opportunity for such statesmanship as does not often grace the courts of emperors and kings!

How we can come to know ourselves, our inmost nature, how we can through this knowledge achieve coordination and our real desires - that is, for Spinoza, the heart of the social problem. The source of man's strength is that he can know his weakness. If he can but find himself out, then he can change himself. "A passion ceases to be a passion as soon as we form a clear and distinct idea of it."[101] When a passion is tracked to its lair and confronted with its futile partiality, its sting is drawn, it can hurt us no more; it may cooperate but it may no longer rule. It is seen to be "inadequate," to express but a fragment of us, and so seen it sinks into its place in the hierarchy of desires. "And in proportion as we know our emotions better, the more are they susceptible to control."[102] Passion is passivity; control is power. Knowledge brings control, and control brings freedom; freedom is not a gift, it is a victory. Knowledge, control, freedom, power, virtue - these are all one thing. Before the "empire of man over nature" must come the empire of man over himself, must come coordination. Achievement is born of clear vision and unified intent, not of actions that are but bubbles on the muddy rapids of desire.

Free Speech

"Before all things, a means must be devised for improving and clarifying the understanding."[103] "Since there is no single thing we know which is more excellent than a man who is guided by reason, it follows that there is nothing by which a person can better show how much skill and talent he possesses than by so educating men that at last they will live under the direct authority of reason."[104] But how?

First of all, says Spinoza, thought must be absolutely free: we must have the possible profit of even the most dangerous heresies. If that proposition appears a trifle trite, let it be remembered that Spinoza wrote at a time when Galileo's broken-hearted retraction was still fresh in men's memories, and when Descartes was modifying his philosophy to soothe the Jesuits. The chapter on freedom of thought is really the pivotal point and *raison d'etre* of the *Tractatus Theologico-Politicus*; and it is still rich in encouragement and inspiration. Perhaps there is nothing else in

---

101. *Ethics*, bk. IV, prop. 3.
102. *Ibid.*, cor.
103. *De Intellectus Emandatione*.
104. *Ethics*, bk. IV, appendix.

Spinoza's writings that is so typical at once of his gentleness and of his strength.

Free speech should be granted, Spinoza argues, because it must be granted. Men may conceal real beliefs, but these same beliefs will inevitably influence their behavior; a belief is not that which is spoken, it is that which is done. A law against free speech is subversive of law itself, for it invites derision from the conscientious. "All laws which can be broken without any injury to another are counted but a laughing-stock."[105] It is useless for the state to command "such things as are abhorrent to human nature." "Men in general are so constituted that there is nothing they will endure with so little patience as that views which they believe to be true should be counted crimes against the law. Under such circumstances men do not think it disgraceful, but most honorable, to hold the laws in abhorrence, and to refrain from no action against the government."[106] Where men are not permitted to criticize their rulers in public, they will plot against them in private. There is no religious enthusiasm stronger than that with which laws are broken by those whose liberty has been suppressed.

Spinoza goes further. Thought must be liberated not only from legal restrictions but from indirect and even unintentional compulsion as well. Spinoza feels very strongly the danger to freedom, that is involved in the organization of education by the state. "Academies that are founded at the public expense are instituted not so much to cultivate men's natural abilities as to restrain them. But in a free commonwealth arts and sciences will be best cultivated to the full if everyone that asks leave is allowed to teach in public, at his own cost and risk."[107] He would have preferred such "freelances" as the Sophists to the state universities of the American Middle West. He did not suggest means of avoiding the apparent alternative of universities subsidized by the rich. It is a problem that has still to be solved.

In demanding absolute freedom of speech Spinoza touches the bases of state organization. Nothing is so dangerous and yet so necessary; for ignorance is the mother of authority. The defenders of free speech have never yet met the contention of such men as Hobbes, that freedom of thought is subversive of established government. The reason is only this: that the contention is probably true, so far as most established governments go. Absolute liberty of speech is assuredly destructive of despotism, no matter how constitutional the despotism may be; and those who have at heart the interests of any such government may be forgiven for hesitating to applaud Spinoza. Freedom of speech makes for social

---

105. *Tractatus Theologico-Politicus*, ch. 10.
106. *Ibid.*, ch. 19.
107. *Ibid.*, ch. 8.

vitality, certainly; without it, indeed, the avenues of mental and social development would be blocked, and life hardly worth living. But freedom of speech cannot be said to make for social stability and permanence, unless the social organization in question invites criticism and includes some mechanism for profiting by it. Where democracy is real, or is on the way to becoming real, free speech will help, not harm, the state; for there is no man so loyal as the man who knows that he may criticize his government freely and to some account. But where there is the autocracy of a person or a class, freedom of speech makes for dissolution, dissolution, however, not of the society so much as of the government. The Bourbons are gone, but France remains. Nay, if the Bourbons had remained, France might be gone.

But to argue today for freedom of speech is to invite the charge of emphasizing the obvious. It may be wholesome to remind ourselves, by a few examples, that however universal the theory of free speech may be, the practice is still rather sporadic. An American professor is dismissed because he thinks there is a plethora of unearned income in his country; an English publicist is reported to have been refused "permission" to fill lecture engagements in America because he had not been sufficiently patriotic; and one of the most prominent of living philosophers loses his chair because he supposes that conscience has rights against cabinets. But indeed our governing bodies are harmless offenders here in comparison with the people themselves. The last lesson which men and women will learn is the lesson of free thought and free speech. The most famous of living dramatists finds himself unsafe in London streets, because he has dared to criticize his government; the most able of living novelists finds it convenient to leave Paris because there are still some Germans whom he does not hate; and an American community full of constitutional lawyers shows its love of "law and order" by stoning a group of boys bent on expounding the desirability of syndicalism.

Perhaps the world has need of many Spinozas still.

Virtue as Power

Freedom of expression is the cornerstone of Spinoza's politics; the postulate without which he refuses to proceed. But Spinoza does not have to be told that this question of free speech precipitates him into the larger problems of "the individual vs. the state"; he knows that that problem is the very *raison d'etre* of political philosophy; he knows that indeed the problem goes to the core of philosophy, arid finds its source and crux in the complex socio-egoistical makeup of the individual man.

The "God-intoxicated" Spinoza is quite sober and disillusioned about the social possibilities of altruism. "It is a universal law of human nature that no one ever neglects anything which he judges to be good, except with the hope of gaining a greater good."[108] "This is as necessarily true as that the whole is greater than its part."[109] This confident reduction of human conduct to self-reference does not for Spinoza involve any condemnation: "reason, since it asks for nothing that is opposed to nature, demands that every person should ... seek his own profit."[110] Observe, reason *demands* this; this same self-seeking is the most valuable and necessary item in the composition of man. Spinoza., as said, goes so far as to identify this self-seeking with virtue: "to act absolutely in conformity with virtue is, in us, nothing but to act, live, and preserve our being (these three have the same meaning) as reason directs, from the ground of seeking our own profit."[111] This is a brave rejection of self-renunciation and asceticism by one whose nature, so far as we can judge it now, inclined him very strongly in the direction of these "virtues". What we have to do, says Spinoza, is not to deny the self, but to broaden it; here again, of course, intelligence is the mother of morals. Progress lies not in self-reduction but in self-expansion. Progress is increase in virtue, but "by virtue and power I understand the same thing";[112] progress is an increase in the ability of men to achieve their ends. It is part of our mental confectionery to define progress in terms of our own ends; a nation is "backward" or "forward" according as it moves towards or away from our own ideals. But that, says Spinoza, is naive nonsense; a nation is progressive or backward according as its citizens are or are not developing greater power to realize their own purposes. That is a doctrine that may have "dangerous" implications, but intelligence will face the implications and the facts, ready not to suppress them but to turn them to account.

It was the passion for power that led to the first social groupings and developed the social instincts. Our varied sympathies, our parental and filial impulses, our heroisms and generosities, all go back to social habits born of individual needs. "Since fear of solitude exists in all men, because no one in solitude is strong enough to defend himself and procure the necessaries of life, it follows that men by nature tend towards social organization."[113] "Let satirists scoff at human affairs as much as they please, let theologians denounce them, and let the melancholy, despising men and admiring brutes, praise as much as they can a life rude and without refinement, men will nevertheless find out that by mutual help they can much more easily procure the things they need, and that it is

---

108. *Tractatus Theologico-Politicus*, ch. 16.

109. *Ethics*, bk. IV, prop. 18.

110. *Ibid.*

111. *Ibid.*, bk. IV, prop. 24.

112. Bk. IV, def. 8.

113. *Tractatus Theologico-Politicus*, ch. 6.

only by their united strength that they can avoid the dangers which everywhere threaten them."[114] *Nihil homine homini utilius.* Men discover that they are useful to one another, and that mutual profit from social organization increases as intelligence grows. In a "state of nature" - that is, before social organization - each man has a "natural right" to do all that he is strong enough to do; in society he yields part of this sovereignty to the communal organization, because he finds that this concession, universalized, increases his strength. The fear of solitude, and not any positive love of fellowship, is the prime force in the origin of society. Man does not join in social organization because he has social instincts; he develops such instincts as the result of joining in such organization.

Freedom and Order

Even today the social instincts are not strong enough to prevent unsocial behavior. "Men are not born fit for citizenship, but must be made so."[115] Hence custom and law. Each man, in his sober moments, desires such social arrangements as will protect him from aggression and interference.[116] "There is no one who does not wish to live, so far as possible, in security and without fear; and this cannot possibly happen so long as each man is allowed to do as he pleases."[117]

"That men who are necessarily subject to passions, and are inconstant and changeable, may be able to live together in security, and to trust one another's fidelity," - that is the purpose of law.[118] Ideally, the state is to the individual what reason is to passion.[119] Law protects a man not only from the passions of others, but from his own; it is a help to delayed response. How to frame laws so that the greatest possible number of men may find their own security and fulfillment in allegiance to the law - that is the problem of the statesman. Law implies force, but so does life, so does nature; indeed, the punishments decreed by "man-made" states are usually milder than those which in a "state of nature" would be the natural consequents of most interferences; not seldom the law - as when it prevents lynching - protects an aggressor from the natural results of his act. Force is the essence of law; hence international law will not really be law until nations are coordinated into a larger group possessed of the instrumentalities of compulsion.[120]

It is clear that Spinoza has the philosophic love of order. "Whatever

---

114. *Ethics*, bk. IV, prop. 35.
115. *Tractatus Theologico-Politicus*, ch. 5 § 2.
116. Durant ultimately credited religion for imposing the social arrangements that allowed civilization to flourish.
117. *Ibid.*, ch. 16.
118. *Ethics*, bk. IV, prop. 37.
119. Contrast Plato: the state (i.e., the governing classes) is to the lower classes as reason is to passion.
120. *Tractatus Theologico-Politicus*, ch. 3 § 4.

conduces to human harmony and fellowship is good; whatever brings discord into the state is evil."[121] But discord, one must repeat, is often the prelude to a greater harmony; development implies variation, and all variation is a discord except to ears that hear the future. The social sanction of liberty lies of course in the potential value of variations; without that vision of new social possibilities (which is suggested by variations from the norm), a people perishes. Spinoza does not see this; but there is a fine passage in the *Tractatus Politicus*[122] which shows him responsive to the ideal of liberty as well as to that of order: "The last end of the state is not to dominate men, nor to restrain them by fear; rather it is so to free each man from fear that he may live and act with full security and without injury to himself or his neighbor. The end of the state is, I repeat, not to make rational beings into brute beasts or machines. It is to enable their bodies and their minds to function safely. It is to lead men to live by, and to exercise, a free reason, that they may not waste their strength in hatred, anger, and guile, not act unfairly toward one another. Thus the end of the state is really liberty."

So it is that Spinoza takes sharp issue with Hobbes and exalts freedom, decentralization, and democracy, where Hobbes, starting with almost identical premises, concludes to a centralized despotism of body and soul. This does not mean that Spinoza had no eye for the defects of democracy. "Experience is supposed to teach that it makes for peace and concord when all authority is conferred upon one man. For no political order has stood so long without notable change as that of the Turks, while none have been so short-lived, nay, so vexed by seditions, as popular or democratic states. But if slavery, barbarism, and desolation are to be called peace, then peace is the worst misfortune that can befall a state. It is true that quarrels are wont to be sharper and more frequent between parents and children than between masters and slaves; yet it advances not the art of home life to change a father's right into a right of property, and count his children as only his slaves. Slavery, then, and not peace, comes from the giving of all power to one man. For peace consists not in the absence of war, but in a union and harmony of men's souls."[123]

No, better the insecurity of freedom than the security of bondage. Better the dangers that come of the ignorance of majorities than those that flow from the concentration of power in the hands of an inevitably self-seeking minority. Even secret diplomacy is worse than the risks of publicity. "It has been the one song of those who thirst after absolute power that the interest of the state requires that its affairs be conducted in secret. But the more such arguments disguise themselves under the

---

121. *Ethics*, bk. IV, prop. 40.
122. Ch. 20.
123. *Tractatus Theologico-Politicus*, ch. 6 § 4.

mask of public welfare the more oppressive is the slavery to which they will lead. Better that right counsels be known to enemies, than that the evil secrets of tyrants should be concealed from the citizens. They who can treat secretly of the affairs of a nation have it absolutely under their authority; and as they plot against the enemy in time of war, so do they against the citizens in time of peace. It is folly to choose to avoid a small loss by means of the greatest of evils."[124]

This is but one of many passages in Spinoza that startle the reader with their present applicability and value. There is in the same treatise a plan for an unpaid citizen soldiery, much like the scheme adopted in Switzerland; there is a plea against centralization and for the development of municipal pride by home rule and responsibility; there is a warning against the danger to democracy involved in the territorial expansion of states; and there is a plan for the state ownership of all land, the rental from this to supply all revenue in time of peace. But let us pass to a more characteristic feature of Spinoza's political theory, and consider with him the function of intelligence in the state.

Democracy and Intelligence

"There is no single thing in nature which is more profitable to man than a man who lives according to the guidance of reason."[125] Such a man, to begin with, has made his peace with the inevitable, and accepts with good cheer the necessary limitations of social life. He has a genial sense of human imperfections, and does not cushion himself upon Utopia. He pursues his own ends but with some perspective of their social bearings; and he is confident that "when each man seeks that which is [really] profitable to himself, then are men most profitable to one another." [126] He knows that the ends of other men will often conflict with his; but he will not for that cause make moral phrases at them. He feels the tragedy of isolated purposes, and knows the worth of cooperation. As he comes to understand the intricate bonds between himself and his fellows he finds ever more satisfaction in purposes that overflow the narrow margins of his own material advantage; until at last he learns to desire nothing for himself without desiring an equivalent for others.[127]

Given such men, democracy follows; such democracy, too, as will be a fulfillment and not a snare. Given such men, penal codes will interest only the antiquarian. Given such men, a society will know the full measure of civic allegiance and communal stability and development. How

---

124. *Tractatus Theologico-Politicus*, ch. 6, § 4, ch. 7 § 9.
125. *Ethics*, bk. IV, prop. 35.
126. *Ibid.*
127. *Ibid.*, prop. 18, schol.; also prop. 37. Cf. Whitman: "By God! I will accept nothing which all cannot have their counterpart of on the same terms."

make such men? By revivals? By the gentle anesthesia of heaven and the cheap penology of hell? By memorizing catechisms and commandments? By appealing like Comte, to the heart, and trusting to the eternal feminine to lead us ever onward? (Onward whither?) Or by spreading the means of intelligence?

It is at this point that the social philosophy of Spinoza, like that of Socrates, betrays its weaker side. How is intelligence to be spread? Perhaps it is too much to ask the philosopher this question; he may feel that he has done enough if he has made clear what it is which will most help us to achieve our ends. Spinoza, after all, was not the kind of man who could be expected to enter into practical problems; his soul was filled with the vision of the eternal laws and had no room for the passing expediencies of action. His devotional geometry was a typical Jewish performance; there is something in the emotional makeup of the Jew which makes him slide very easily into the attitude of worship, as contrasted with the Greco-Roman emphasis on intellect and control. All pantheism tends to quietism; to see things *sub specie eternitatis* may very well pass from the attitude of the scientist to the attitude of the mystic who has no interest in temporal affairs. It is the task of philosophy to study the eternal and universal not for its own sake but for its worth in directing us through the maze of temporal particulars; the philosopher must be like the mariner who guides himself through space and time by gazing at the everlasting stars. It is wholesome that the history of philosophy should begin with Thales; so that all who come to the history of philosophy may learn, at the door of their subject, that though stars are beautiful, wells are deep.

The Legacy of Spinoza

But to leave the matter thus would be to lose a part of the truth in the glare of one's brilliance. We have to recognize that though Spinoza stopped short (or rather was cut short) at merely a statement of the prime need of all democracies - *intelligence* - he was nevertheless the inspiration of men who carried his beginning more nearly to a practical issue. To Spinoza, through Voltaire and the English deists, one may trace not a few of the thought-currents which carried away the foundations of ecclesiastical power, civil and intellectual, in eighteenth-century France, and left the middle class conscience-free to engineer a revolution. It was from Spinoza chiefly that Rousseau derived his ideas of popular sovereignty, of the general will, of the right of revolution, of the legitimacy of the force that makes men free, and of the ideal state as that in which all the citizens

---

128. Not that these ideas were original with Spinoza; they were the general legacy of Renaissance political thought. But it was through the writings of Spinoza that this legacy was transmitted to Rousseau. *Cf.* Duff. p. 319.

form an assembly with final power.[128] The French Declaration of Rights and the American Declaration of Independence go back in part to the forgotten treatises of the quiet philosopher of Amsterdam. To have initiated or accelerated such currents of thought - theoretical in their origin but extremely practical in their issue - is thereby once for all to have put one's self above the reach of mere fault-finding. One wonders again, as so many have wondered, what would have been the extent of this man's achievement had he not died at the age of 44. When Spinoza's pious landlady returned from church on the morning of February 21, 1677, and found her gentle philosopher dead, she stood in the presence of one of the great silent tragedies of human history.

CHAPTER FIVE
NIETZSCHE

From Spinoza to Nietzsche

Let us dare to compress within a page or two the social aspect of philosophical thought from Spinoza to Nietzsche. Without forgetting that our purpose is to show the social problem as the dominant interest of only *many*, not all, of the greater philosophers, we may yet risk the assertion that the majority of the men who formed the epistemological tradition from Descartes to Kant were at heart concerned less with the problem of knowledge than with that of social relations. Descartes slips through this generalization; he is a man of leisure lost in the maze of a puzzle which he has not discovered so much as he has unconsciously constructed it. In Locke's hands the puzzle is distorted into the question of "innate ideas," in order that, under cover of an innocent epistemological excursion, a blow may be struck at hereditary prejudices and authoritarian teaching, and the way made straight for the advance of popular sovereignty (as against; the absolutism of Hobbes), free speech, reasonable religion, and social amelioration. The dominance of the social interest is not so easily shown in the case of Leibniz; but let it be remembered none the less that epistemology was but an aside in the varied drama of Leibniz' life, and that his head was dizzy with schemes for the betterment of this "best of all possible worlds." Bishop Berkeley begins with *esse est percipi* and ends with tarwater as the *solution* of all problems. David Hume, in the midst of a life busied with politics and the discussion of social, political, and economic problems, spares a year or two for epistemology, only to use it as a handle whereby to deal a blow to dogma; he "was more damaging to religion than Voltaire, but was ingenious enough not to get the credit for it."[129] The social incidence of philosophy in eighteenth-century France was so decided that one might describe that philosophy as part of the explosive with which the middle class undermined the *status quo*. This social emphasis continues in Comte; who cannot forget that he was once the secretary of St. Simon, and will not let us forget that the function of the philosopher is to coordinate experience with a view to the remolding of human life. John Stuart Mill is radical first and logician afterward; and the more lasting as well as the more interesting element in Spencer is the sociological, educational, and political theory.

---

129. Professor Woodbridge, class lecture.

In Kant the basic social interest is buried under epistemological cobwebs, yet not so choked but that it finds very resolute voice at last. The essence of the matter here is the return of the prodigal, the relapse of a once adventurous soul into the comfort of religious and political absolutes, categorical - and Potsdam - imperatives. Here is "dogmatic slumber" overcome only to yield to the torpor and *abetisement* of "practical reason"; here is no "Copernican revolution" but a stealthy attempt to recover an anthropocentricism lost in the glare of the Enlightenment. It dawns on us that the importance of German philosophy is not metaphysical, nor epistemological, but political; the vital remnant of Kant today is to be found not in our overflowing Mississippi of Kantiana, but in the German notion of obedience.[130] Fichte reinforces this notion of unquestioning obedience with the doctrine of state socialism: he begins by tending geese, and ends by writing philosophy for them. So with Hegel: he starts out buoyantly with the proposition that revolution is the heart of history, and ends by discovering that the King of Prussia is God in disguise. In Schopenhauer the bubble bursts; a millennium of self-deception ends at last in exhaustion and despair. Every Hildebrand has his Voltaire, and every Voltaire his Schopenhauer.

Biographical

"In future," Nietzsche once wrote, "let no one concern himself about me, but only about the things for which I lived." We must make this biographical note brief.

Nietzsche was born in Rocken, Germany, 1844, the son of a "noble young parson." He was brought up in strict piety, and prepared himself to enter the ministry; even at boarding-school he was called "the little minister," and made people cry by his recitations from the Bible. We have pictures of him which show him in all his boyish seriousness; it is evident that he is of a deeply religious nature, and therefore doomed to heresy. At eighteen he discovers that he has begun to doubt the traditional creed. "When I examine my own thoughts," he writes, "and hearken into my own soul, I often feel as if I heard the buzzing and roaring of wild-contending parties."[131] At 21, while studying in the University of Leipzig, he discovers the philosophy of Schopenhauer; he reads all hungrily, feeling here a kindred youth, "the need of knowing myself, even of gnawing at myself, forcibly seized upon me."[132] He is ripe for pessimism, having both religion and a bad stomach. Because of his defective eyesight he is barred from military service; in 1870 he burns with patriotic fever, and at last is allowed

130. Cf. Professor Dewey's *German Philosophy and Politics*, New York, 1916.
131. Forster-Nietzsche, *The Young Nietszche*, London, 1912, p. 98.
132. *Ibid.*, p. 152.

to join the army as a nurse; but he is almost overcome at sight of the sick and wounded, and himself falls ill with dysentery and dyspepsia. In this same year he sees a troop of cavalry pass through a town in stately gallop and array; his weakened frame thrills with the sight of this strength: "I felt for the first time that the strongest and highest Will to Life does not find expression in a miserable struggle for existence, but in a Will to War, a Will to Power, a Will to Overpower!"[133] Nevertheless, he settles down to a quietly ascetic life as professor of philology at the University of Basle. But there is adventure in him; and in his first book[134] he slips from the prose of philology into an almost lyrical philosophy. Illness finds voice here in the eulogy of health, weakness in the deification of strength, melancholy in the praise of "Dionysian joy", loneliness in the exaltation of friendship. He has a friend - Wagner - the once romantic rebel of revolution's barricades; but this friend too is taken from him, with slowly painful breaking of bond after bond. For Wagner, the strong, the overbearing, the ruthless, is coming to a philosophy of Christian sympathy and gentleness, qualities that cannot seem divine to Nietzsche, because they are long-familiar elements in his own character. "What I am not," he says, most truthfully, "that for me is God and virtue."[135] And so he stands at last alone, borne up solely by the exhilaration of creative thought. He has acquaintances, but he puts up with them "simply, like a patient animal"; "not one has the faintest inkling of my task." And he suffers terribly "through this absence of sympathy and understanding."[136]

He leaves even these acquaintances, and abandons his work at Basle; broken in health he finds his way hopefully to the kindlier climate of Italy. Doctor after doctor prescribes for him, one prescription reading, "a nice Italian sweetheart." He longs for the comradeship, but dreads the friction, of marriage. "It seems to me absurd," he writes, "that one who has chosen for his sphere . . . the assessment of existence as a whole, should burden himself with the cares of a family, with winning bread, security, and social position for wife and children." He does not hesitate to conclude that "where the highest philosophical thinking is concerned all married men are suspect."[137] Nevertheless he wanders humanly into something very like a love-affair; he is almost shattered with rapid disillusionment, and takes refuge in philosophy. "Every misunderstanding," he tells himself, "has made me freer. I want less and less from humanity, and can give it more and more. The severance of every individual tie is hard to bear; but in each case a wing grows in its place."[138] And yet the need

---

133. *Ibid.*, p. 235
134. *The Birth of Tragedy*, 1872.
135. *Thus Spake Zarathustra*, p. 129.
136. Forster-Nietszche, *The Lonely Nietszche*, London, 1915, pp. 77, 212, 291.
137. *Ibid.*, p. 313.
138. *Ibid.*, p. 181.

of comradeship is still there, like a gnawing hunger: many years later he catches a passing smile from a beautiful young woman, whom he has never seen before; and "suddenly my lonely philosopher's heart grew warm within me."[139] But she walks off without seeing him, and they never meet again.

The simple Italians who rent him his attic room in Genoa understand him better perhaps than he can be understood by more pretentious folk. They know his greatness, though they cannot classify it. The children of his landlady call him "Il Santo"; and the market-women keep their choicest grapes for the bent philosopher who, it is whispered, writes bitterly about women and "the superfluous." But what they know for certain is that he is a man of exceeding gentleness and purity, that he is the very soul of chivalry; "stories are still told of his politeness towards women to whom no one else showed any kindness."[140] Let him write what he pleases, so long as he is what he is.

He lives simply, almost in poverty. "His little room," writes a visitor, "is bare and cheerless. It has evidently been selected for cheapness rather than for comfort. No carpet, not even a stove. I found it fearfully cold."[141] His publisher has made no profit on his books; they are too sharply opposed to the "spirit of the age", hence the title he gives to two of his volumes: *Unzeitgemasse Betrachtungen - Thoughts Out of Season*. There is no money, he is now informed, in such untimely volumes; hereafter he must publish his books at his own cost. He does, stinting himself severely to meet the new expense; his greatest books see the light in this way.[142]

He works hard, knowing that his shaken frame has but short lease of life; and he comes to love his painful solitude as a gift. "I can't help seeing an enemy in anyone who breaks in upon my working summer. The idea that any person should intrude upon the web of thought which I am spinning around me, is simply appalling. I have no more time to lose - unless I am stingy with my precious *half-hours* I shall have a bad conscience."[143] Half-hours; his eyes will not work for more than thirty minutes at a time. He feels that only to him to whom time is holy does time bring reward. "He is fully convinced," an acquaintance writes of him, "about his mission and his permanent importance. In this belief he is strong and great; it elevates him above all misfortune." He speaks of his *Thus Spake*

139. *Ibid.*, p. 297.
140. *Ibid.*, p. 424.
141. *Ibid.*, p. 195.
142. Chronology of Nietszche's chief works, With initials used in subsequent references: *Thoughts Out of Season* ("T. O. S.") (1873-6); *Human All Too Human* ("H. H.") (1876-80); *Dawn of Day* ("D. D.") (1881); *Joyful Wisdom* ("J. W.") (1882); *Thus Spake Zarathustra* (" Z.") (1883-4); *Beyond Good and Evil* ("B. G. E.") (1886); *Genealogy of Morals* ("G. M.") (1887); *Twilight of the Idols* ("T.I.") (1888); *Antichrist* ("Antich."); *Ecce Homo* ("E. H."), and *Will to Power* ("W. P.") (1889).
143. *Lonely N*, p. 104.
144. *Ibid.*, p. 195.

Zarathustra in terms of almost conscious exaggeration: "It is a book," he says, "that stands alone. Do not let us mention the poets in the same breath; nothing perhaps has ever been produced out of such a super-abundance of strength."[145] He does not know that it is his illness and his hunger for appreciation that have demanded this self-laudation as restorative and nourishment. He predicts, rightly enough, that he will not begin to get his due meed of appreciation till 1901.[146] His "unmasking of Christian morality," he says, "is an event unequalled in history."[147]

All this man's energy is in his brain; he oozes ideas at every pore. He crowds into a sentence the material of a chapter; and every aphorism is a mountain peak. He dares to say that which others dare only to think, and we call him witty because truth tabooed is the soul of wit. Every page bears the imprint of the passion and the pain that gave it birth. "I am not a man," he says, "I am dynamite"; he writes like a man who feels error after error exploding at his touch, and he defines a philosopher as "a terrible explosive in the presence of which everything is in danger."[148] "There are more idols than realities in the world; and I have an 'evil eye' for idols."[149]

What is this philosophy which seemed to its creator more important than even the mightiest events of the past? How shall we compress it without distorting it, as it has been distorted by so many of its lovers and its haters? Let us ask the man himself to speak to us; let us see if we cannot put the matter in his own words, ourselves but supplying, so to speak, connective tissue. That done, we shall understand the man better, and ourselves, and perhaps our social problem.

EXPOSITION[150]

Morality as Impotence

From a biological standpoint the phenomenon morality is of a highly suspicious nature.[151] *Cui bono* - Whom shall we suspect of profiting by this institution? Is it a mode of enhancing life? - Does it make men stronger and more perfect? - or does it make for deterioration and decay? It is obvious that up to the present, morality has not been a problem at all; it has rather been the very ground on which people have met after all dis-

---

145. *E. H.*, p. 106.
146. *J. W.*, § 371.
147. *E. H.*, p. 141.
148. *Ibid.*, pp. 131, 81.
149. *T. I.*, pref.
150. It is at this point that Durant begins to outline the philosophy of Nietzsche, not his own. To the lay reader, this transition may not be immediately obvious, but there are striking differences between the philosophy of Nietzsche and the Perspectivism of Will Durant.
151. *W. P.* § 400.

trust, dissension, and contradiction, the hallowed place of peace, where thinkers could obtain rest even from themselves.[152] But what if morality be the greatest of all the stumbling blocks in the way of human self-betterment? Is it possible that morality itself is the social problem, and that the solution of that problem lies in the judicious abolition of morality? It is a view for which something can be said.

You have heard that morality is a means used by the strong to control the weak. And it is true: just consider the conversion of Constantine. But to stop here is to let half the truth be passed off on you as the whole; and half a truth is half a lie. Much more true is it that morality is a means used by the weak to control the strong, the chain which weakness softly lays upon the feet of strength. The whole of the morality of Europe is based upon the values which are useful to the herd.[153] Every one's desire is that there should be no other teaching and valuation of things than those by means of which he himself succeeds. Thus the fundamental tendency of the weak and mediocre of all times has been to enfeeble the strong and to reduce them to the level of the weak; their chief weapon in this process was the moral principle.[154] Good is every one who does not oppress, who hurts no one, attacks no one, does not take vengeance but hands over vengeance to God; who goes out of the way of evil, and demands little from life; like ourselves, patient, meek, just. Good is to do nothing for which we are not strong enough.[155] Zarathustra laughed many times over the weaklings who thought themselves good because they had lame paws![156] Obedience, subordination, submission, devotion, love, the pride of duty; fatalism, resignation, objectivity, stoicism, asceticism, self-denial; in short, anemia: these are the virtues which the herd would have all men cultivate - particularly the strong men.[157] And the deification of Jesus, that is to say of meekness - what was it but another attempt to lull the strong to sleep?

See, now, how nearly that attempt has succeeded. For is not democracy, if not victorious, at least on the road to victory today? And what is the democratic movement but the inheritor of Christianity?[158] Not the Christianity of the great popes; they knew better, and were building a splendid aristocracy when Luther spoiled it all by letting loose the leveling instincts of the herd.[159] The instinct of the herd is in favor of the leveler (Christ).[160] I very much fear that the first Christian is in his deepest

---

152. *J. W.* § 345.
153. *W.P.* § 276.
154. *Ibid.*, § 345.
155. *G. M.*, p. 46.
156. *Z.* p. 166.
157. *W. P.* § 721; *T. I.* p. 89.
158. *B. G. E.* § 202.
159. *J. W.* § 358; *Antich.* § 361.
160. *W. P.* § 284.

instincts a rebel against everything privileged; he lives and struggles unremittingly for "equal rights."[161] It is by Christianity, more than by anything else, that the poison of this doctrine of "equal rights" has been spread abroad. And do not let us underestimate the fatal influence! Nowadays no one has the courage of special rights, of rights of dominion. The aristocratic attitude of mind has been most thoroughly undermined by the lie of the equality of souls.[162]

But is not this the greatest of all lies - the "equality of men"? That is to say, the dominion of the inferior. Is it not the most threadbare and discredited of ideas? Democracy represents the disbelief in all great men and select classes; everybody equals everybody else; "at bottom we are all herd." There is no welcome for the genius here; the more promising for the future the modern individual happens to be, the more suffering falls to his lot.[163] If the rise of great and rare men had been made dependent upon the voices of the multitude, there never would have been any such thing as a great man. The herd regards the exception, whether it be above or beneath its general level, as something antagonistic and dangerous. Their trick in dealing with the exceptions above them - the strong, the mighty, the wise, the fruitful - is to persuade them to become their head-servants.[164]

But the torture of the exceptional soul is only part of the villainy of democracies. The other part is chaos. Voltaire was right: "*Quand la populace se mele de raisonner, tout est perdu.*" Democracy is an aristocracy of orators, a competition in headlines, a maelstrom of ever new majorities, a torrent of petty factions sweeping on to ruin. Under democracy the state will decay, for the instability of legislation will leave little respect for law, until finally even the policeman will have to be replaced by private enterprise.[165] Democracy has always been the death agony of the power of organization:[166] remember Athens, and look at England. Within fifty years these Babel governments will clash in a gigantic war for the control of the markets of the world; and when that war comes, England will pay the penalty for the democratic inefficiency of its dominant muddle-class.[167]

This wave of democracy will recede, and recede quickly, if men of ability will only oppose it openly. It is necessary for higher men to declare war on the masses. In all directions mediocre people are joining hands in order to make themselves master. The middle classes must be dissolved,

---

161. *Antich.*, § 46.
162. *Ibid.,* § 43.
163. *W.P.,* § 464, 861, 748, 752, 686.
164. *Ibid.,* § 885, 281.
165. *H. H.,* § 428, 472.
166. *T. I. P.,* 96.
167. *G. M.,* p. 225.

and their influence decreased;[168] there must be no more intermarrying of aristocracy with plutocracy; this democratic folly would never have come at all had not the master classes allowed their blood to be mingled with that of slaves.[169] Let us fight parliamentary government and the power of the press; they are the means whereby cattle become rulers.[170] Finally, it is senseless and dangerous to let the counting-mania (the custom of universal suffrage) - which is still but a short time under cultivation, and could easily be uprooted - take deeper root; its introduction was merely an expedient to steer clear of temporary difficulties; the time is ripe for a demonstration of democratic incompetence and a restoration of power to men who are born to rule.[171]

Feminism[172]

Democracy, after all, is a disease; an attempt on the part of the botched to lay down for all the laws of social health. You may observe the disease in its growth process by studying the woman movement. Woman's first and last function is that of bearing robust children.[173] The emancipated ones are the abortions among women, those who lack the wherewithal to have children (I go no farther, lest I should become medicynical).[174] All intellect in women is a pretension; when a woman has scholarly inclinations there is generally something wrong with her sex. These women think to make themselves charming to free spirits by wearing advanced views; as though a woman without piety would not be something perfectly obnoxious and ludicrous to a profound and godless man![175] If there is anything worthy of laughter it is the man who takes part in this feminist agitation. Let it be understood clearly that the relations between men and women make equality impossible. It is in the nature of woman to take color and commandment from a man - unless she happens to be a man. Man's happiness is "I will," woman's happiness is "He will."[176] Woman gives herself, man takes her: I do not think one will get over this natural contrast by any social contract.[177] Indeed, women will lose power with every step towards emancipation. Since the French

---

168. *W. P.*, § 861, 891.
169. *B. G. E.*, p. 233.
170. *W. P.*, § 753.
171. *G. M.*, p. 223.
172. The subject of feminism is an area in which Will Durant fervently disagreed with Nietzsche. While Nietzsche's misogynistic tendencies permeated his philosophy, Durant was very progressive in his belief in women's equal rights. It is important to reassert that the views presented in this passage are Nietzsche's and not Durant's.
173. *B. G. E.*, p. 189.
174. *E. H.*, p. 65.
175. *B. G. E.*, pp. 96, 189.
176. *Z. P.*, 89.
177. *J. W.*, § 363.

Revolution the influence of woman has declined in proportion as she has increased her rights and claims. Let her first do her proper work properly (consider how much man has suffered from stupidity in the kitchen), and then it may be time to consider an extension of her activities. To be mistaken in this fundamental problem of "man and woman," to deny here the profoundest antagonism, and the necessity for an eternally hostile tension, to dream here of equal rights, equal training, equal claims and obligations: that is a typical sign of shallow-mindedness. On the other hand, a man who has depth of spirit as well as of desires, and has also the depth of benevolence which is capable of severity and harshness, and easily confounded with them, can only think of woman as Orientals do: he must conceive of her as a possession, as confinable property, as a being predestined for service and accomplishing her mission therein - he must take his stand in this matter upon the immense rationality of Asia, upon the superiority of the instincts of Asia.[178]

Socialism and Anarchism

All this uprising of housekeepers is, of course, part of the general sickness with which Christianity has inoculated and weakened the strong races of Europe. Consider now the more virulent forms of the disease: socialism and anarchism.[179] The coming of the "kingdom of God" has here been placed in the future, and been given an earthly, a human, meaning; but on the whole the faith in the old ideal is still maintained. There is still the comforting delusion about equal rights, with all the envy that lurks in that delusion. One speaks of "equal rights": that is to say, so long as one is not a dominant personality, one wishes to prevent one's competitors from growing in power.[180] It is a pleasure for all poor devils to grumble - it gives them a little intoxicating sensation of power. There is a small dose of revenge in every lamentation.[181] When you hear one of those reformers talk of humanity, you must not take him seriously; it is only his way of getting fools to believe that he is an altruist; beneath the cover of this buncombe a man strong in the gregarious instincts makes his bid for fame and followers and power. This pretense to altruism is only

---

178. *B. G. E.*, pp. 188, 184, 189.
179. Again, Durant and Nietzsche could not be philosophically further apart on this issue. Durant was a vocal and committed socialist at this point in his life and had a respect for anarchism stemming from both his years of teaching for the anarchist Ferrer Modern School and the kindness of his benefactor, Alden Freeman, who was an anarchist.
   Durant described the anarchists in his 1927 book *Transitions*: "What did these people mean by anarchism? To the outside world, and to a certain 'lunatic fringe' within the group itself, the word meant the approval of any means, moral or physical, peaceful or violent, that the exploited classes might care to use in their war for freedom. But to the finer spirits in the movement, anarchism meant just the opposite of this: it was the absolute rejection of physical force as unnecessary in human affairs." (Source: *Transitions*, p. 191.)
180. *W. P.*, § 339, 86.
181. *T. I.*, p. 86.

a roundabout way of asking for altruism, it is the result of a consciousness of the fact that one is botched and bungled.[182] In short, socialism is not justice but covetousness.[183] No doubt we should look upon its exponents and followers with ironic compassion: they want something which we have.[184]

From the standpoint of natural science the highest conception of society according to socialists is the lowest in the order of rank among societies. A socialist community would be another China, a vast and stifling mediocracy; it would be the tyranny of the lowest and most brainless brought to its zenith.[185] A nation in which there would be no exploitation would be dead. Life itself is essentially appropriation, conquest of the strange and weak; to put it at its mildest, exploitation.[186] The absence of exploitation would mean the end of organic functioning. Surely it is as legitimate and valuable for superior men to command and use inferior men as it is for superior species to command and use inferior species, as man commands and uses animals.[187] It is not surprising that the lamb should bear a grudge against the great birds of prey, but that is no reason for blaming the great birds of prey.[188] What should be done with muscle except to supply it with directive brains? How, otherwise, can anything worthy ever be built by men? In fact, man has value and significance only in so far as he is a stone in a great building; for which purpose he has first of all to be solid; he has to be a "stone."[189]

Now the common people understand this quite well, and are as happy as any of the well-to-do, so long as a silly propaganda does not disturb them with dreams that can never be fulfilled.[190] Poverty, cheerfulness, and independence - it is possible to find these three qualities combined in one individual; poverty, cheerfulness, and slavery - this is likewise a possible combination: and I can say nothing better to the workmen who serve as factory-slaves.[191]

As for the upper classes, they need be at no loss for weapons with which to fight this pestilence. An occasional opening of the trapdoor between the *Haves* and the *Have-nots*, increasing the number of property owners, will serve best of all. If this policy is pursued, there will always be too many people of property for socialism ever to signify anything more than an attack of illness.[192] A little patience with inheritance and

182. *J. W.*, § 377; *W. P.*, § 350, 315, 373.
183. *H. H.*, § 451.
184. *W. P.*, § 761.
185. *Ibid.*, § 51, 125.
186. *B. G. B.*, p. 226.
187. *W. P.*, § 856.
188. *G. M.*, p. 44.
189. *J. W.*, § 356.
190. *Lonely N.*, p. 83.
191. *D. D.*, § 206.
192. *W. P.*, § 125.

income taxes, and the noise of the cattle will subside.[193]

Notice, meanwhile, that socialism and despotism are bedfellows. Give the socialist his way, and he will put everything into the hands of the state - that is to say, into the hands of demagogue politicians.[194] And then, all in the twinkling of an eye, socialism begets its opposite in good Hegelian fashion, and the dogs of anarchism are let loose to till the world with their howling. And not without excuse or benefit; for politicians must be kept in their place, and the state rigidly restricted to its necessary functions, even if anarchist agitation helps one to do it.[195] And the anarchists are right: the state is the coldest of all monsters, and this lie creeps out of its mouth, "I, the State, am the people."[196] So the wise man will turn anarchism, as well as socialism, to account; and he will not fret even when a king or two is hurried into heaven with nitroglycerine. Only since they have been shot at have princes once more sat securely on their thrones.[197]

Anarchism justifies itself in the aristocrat, who feels law as his instrument, not as his master; but the rebellion against law as such is but one more outburst of physiological misfits bent on leveling and revenge.[198] It is childish to desire a society in which every individual would have as much freedom as another.[199] Decadence speaks in the democratic idiosyncrasy against everything which rules and wishes to rule, the modern *misarchism* (to coin a bad word for a bad thing).[200] When all men are strong enough to command, then law will be superfluous; weakness needs the vertebrae of law. He is commanded who cannot obey his own self. Let the anarchist be thankful that he has laws to obey. To command is more difficult; whenever living things command they risk themselves; they take the hard responsibilities for the result.[201] Freedom is the will to be responsible for ourselves;[202] when the mob is capable of that, it will be time to think of dispensing with law. The truth is, of course, that the anarchist is lulled into nonsense by Rousseau's notion of the naturally good man. He does not understand that revolution merely unleashes the dogs in man, till they once more cry for the whip.[203] Cast out the Bourbons and in ten years you will welcome Napoleon.

That is the end of anarchism; and it is the end of democracy, too.

The truth is that men are willing and anxious to be ruled by rulers wor-

---

193. *Wonder and His Shadow*, 292 (*H. H.*, II, p. 343).
194. *H. H.*, I, § 473.
195. *D. D.*, § 179.
196. *Z.*, p. 62.
197. *W. P.*, § 329.
198. *T. I.*, p. 86; *E. H.*, p. 66; *Antich.*, § 57.
199. *W. P.*, § 859.
200. *G. M.*, p. 91.
201. *Z.*, p. 159.
202. *T. I.*, p. 94.
203. *H. H.*, § 463.

thy of the name. But the corrupted ruling classes have brought ruling into evil odor. The degeneration of the ruler and of the ruling classes has been the cause of all the disorders in history. Democracy is not ruling, but drifting; it is a political relaxation, as if an organism were to allow each of its parts to do just as it pleased. Precisely these disorganizing principles give our age its specific character. Our society has lost the power to function properly; it no longer rids itself naturally of its rotten elements; it no longer has the strength even to excrete.[204]

Degeneration

What kind of men is to be found in such a society? Mediocre men, men stupid to the point of sanctity, fragile, useless souls-de-luxe, men suffering from a sort of hemiplegia of virtue - that is to say, paralyzed in the self-assertive instincts, men tamed, almost emasculated by a morality whose essence is the abdication of the will.[205] Now, as a rule, the taming of a beast is achieved only by deteriorating it; so too the moral man is not a better man, he is rather a weaker member of his species. He is altruistic, of course - that is, he feels that he needs help. There is no place for really great men in this march towards nonentity; if a great man appears he is called a criminal.[206] A Periclean Greek, a Renaissance Florentine, would breathe like one asphyxiated in this moralic acid atmosphere; the first condition of life for such a man is that he free himself from this Chinadom of the spirit.[207] But the number of those who are capable of rising into the pure air of unmoralism is very small, and those who have made timid sallies into theological heresy are the most addicted to the comfort and security of ethical orthodoxy. In short, men are coming to look upon lowered vitality as the heart of virtue, and morality will be saddled with the guilt if the maximum potentiality of the power and splendor of the human species should never be attained.[208]

Men of this stamp require a good deal of religious pepsin to overcome the indigestibility of life; if they leave one faith in the passing bravery of their youth they soon sink back into another.[209] God, previously diluted from tribal deity into *substantia* and *ding-an-sich*,[210] now recovers a respectable degree of reality; the imaginary pillar on which men lean is made stronger and more concrete as their weakness increases. How much faith a person requires in order to flourish, how much fixed opinion he needs which he does not wish to have shaken, because he holds him-

204. *W. P.*, § 750, 874, 65, 50.
205. *B. G. E.*, p. 173; *W. P.*, § 823, 851, 871, 11.
206. *W. P.*, § 397, 12, 736.
207. *E. H.*, p. 136.
208. *G. M.*, p. 10.
209. *T. O. S., I*, p. 78.0.
210. *Antich.*, § 17.

self thereby, is a measure of his power (or more plainly speaking, of his weakness).[211]

The same criterion classifies our friends the metaphysicians - those albinos of thought - who are, of course, priests in disguise.[212] The degree of a man's willpower may be measured by the extent to which he can dispense with the meaning in things, by the extent to which he is able to endure a world without meaning, because he himself arranges a small portion of it.[213] The world has no meaning; all the better; put some meaning into it, says the man with a man's heart. The world has no meaning; but it is only a world of appearance, says the weak-kneed philosopher; behind this phenomenal world is the real world, which has meaning, and means good. Of the real world "there is no knowledge; consequently there is a God" - what novel elegance of syllogism![214] This belief that the world which ought to be is real is a belief proper to the unfruitful who do not wish to create a world. The "will to truth" is the impotence of the "will to create."[215] Even monism is being turned into medicine for sick souls; clearly these lovers of wisdom seek not truth, but remedies for their illnesses.[216] There is too much beer and midnight oil in modern philosophy, and not enough fresh air.[217] Philosophers condemn this world because they have avoided it; those who are contemplative naturally belittle activity.[218] In truth, the history of philosophy is the story of a secret and mad hatred of the prerequisites of life, of the feelings which make for the real values of life.[219] No wonder that philosophy is fallen to such low estate. Science flourishes nowadays, and has the good conscience clearly visible on its countenance; while the remnant to which modern philosophy has gradually sunk excites distrust and displeasure, if not scorn and pity. Philosophy reduced to a "theory of knowledge," a philosophy that never gets beyond the threshold, and rigorously denies itself the right to enter - that is philosophy in its last throes, an end, an agony; something that awakens pity. How could such a philosophy rule![220]

Nihilism

All these things, democracy, feminism, socialism, anarchism, and modern philosophy, are heads of the Christian hydra, each a sore in the total disease. Given such illness, affecting all parts of the social body, and

---

211. *J. W.*, § 347.
212. *Antich.*, § 17.
213. *W. P.*, § 585.
214. *G. M.*, p. 202.
215. *W. P.*, § 585.
216. *Ibid.*, § 600; *D. D.*, 424.
217. *J. W.*, § 366.
218. *D. D.*, § 41.
219. *W. P.*, § 461.
220. *B. G. E.*, p. 136.

what result shall we expect and find? Pessimism, despair, nihilism - that is, disbelief in all values of life.[221] Confidence in life is gone; life itself has become a problem. Love of life is still possible - only it is the love of a woman of whom one is doubtful.[222] The "good man" sees himself surrounded by evil, discovers traces of evil in every one of his acts. And thus he ultimately arrives at the conclusion, which to him is quite logical, that nature is evil, that man is corrupted, and that being good is an act of grace (that is to say, it is impossible to man when he stands alone). In short, *he denies life*.[223] The man who frees himself from the theology of the Church but adheres to Christian ethics necessarily falls into pessimism. He perceives that man is no longer an assistant in, let alone the culmination of, the evolutionary process; he perceives that Becoming has been aiming at Nothing, and has achieved it, and that is something which he cannot bear.[224] Suffering, which was, before, a trial with promised reward, is now an intolerable mystery; if he is materially comfortable himself, he finds source for sentiment and tears in the pain and misery of others; he concocts a "social problem," and never dreams that the social problem is itself a result of decadence.[225] He does not feel at home in this world in which the Christian God is dead, and to which, nevertheless, he brings nothing more appreciative than the old Christian moral attitude. He despairs because he is a chaos, and knows it; "I do not know where I am, or what I am to do; I am everything that knows not where it is or what to do," he sighs.[226] Life, he says at last, is not worth living.

Let us not try to answer such a man; he needs not logic but a sanitarium. But see, through him, and in him, the destructiveness of Christian morals.[227] This despicable civilization, says Rousseau, is to blame for our bad morality. What if our good morality is to blame for this despicable civilization?[228] See how the old ethic depreciates the joy of living, and the gratitude felt towards life, how it checks the knowledge and unfolding of life, how it chokes the impulse to beautify and ennoble life.[229] And at what a time! Think what a race with masculine will could accomplish now! Precisely now, when will in its fullest strength were necessary, it is in the weakest and most pusillanimous condition. Absolute mistrust concerning

---

221. *W. P.*, § 8.
222. *J. W.*, p. 7.
223. *W. P.*, § 351.
224. *Ibid.*, § 12.
225. *Ibid.*, § 43.
226. *Antich.*, § 1.
227. Again, this perspective of Nietzsche departs greatly from Will Durant's personal philosophy. One of Durant's core philosophical arguments was that religion was necessary for the development and progress of civilization; that, without it, man would have remained in a state of barbarism. So for Durant, religion and the morality it imposed on people is the reason that our evolved civilization exists. It should also be noted that while he was an atheist, Durant's fondness for his former faith was unabated, with his wife Ariel frequently referring to him as "Catholic from the neck down".
228. *D. D.*, § 163.
229. *W. P.*, § 266.

the organizing power of the will: to that we have come.[230] The world is dark with despair at the moment of greatest light.

What if man could be made to: love the light and use it?

The Will to Power

Is it possible that this despair is not the final state in the exhaustion of a race, but only a transition from belief in a perfect and ethical world to an attitude of transvaluation and control?[231] Perhaps we are at the bottom of our spiritual toboggan, and an ascending movement is around the comer of the years. Now that our Christian bubble has burst into Schopenhauer, we are left free to recover some part of the joyous strength of the ancients. Let us become again as little children, unspoiled by religion and morality; let us forget what it is to feel sinful; let the thousandfold laughter of children clear the air of the odor of decay. Let us begin anew and the soul will rise and overflow all its margins with the joy of rediscovered life.[232] Life has not deceived us! On the contrary, from year to year it appears richer, more desirable, and more mysterious; the old fetters are broken by the thought that life may be an experiment and not a duty, not a fatality, not a deceit![233] Life - that means for us to transform constantly into light and flame all that we are, and also all that we meet with - we cannot possibly do otherwise.[234] To be natural again, to dare to be as immoral as nature is, to be such pagans as were the Greeks of the Homeric age, to say Yea to life, even to its suffering, to win back some of that mountain-air Dionysian spirit which took pleasure in the tragic, nay, which invented tragedy as the expression of its superabundant vitality, as the expression of its welcome of even the cruelest and most terrible elements of life![235] To be healthy once more!

For there is no other virtue than health, vigor, energy. All virtues should be looked upon as physiological conditions, and moral judgments are symptoms of physiological prosperity or the reverse. Indeed, it might be worthwhile to try to see whether a scientific order of values might not be constructed according to a scale of numbers and measures representing energy. All other values are matters of prejudice, simplicity, and misunderstanding.[236] Instead of moral values let us use naturalistic values, physiological values; let us say frankly with Spinoza that virtue and power are one and the same. What is good? All that enhances the feeling of power, the will to power, and power itself, in man. What is bad? All

---

230. *Ibid.*, § 20.
231. *Ibid.*, § 585.
232. *Z.*, pp. 193,316; *E. H.*, pp. 71, 28.
233. *J. W.*, § 324.
234. *Ibid.*, p. 6.
235. *W. P.*, § 120, 1029., *Antich.* § 55; *E. H.*, pp. 72, 70; *Birth of Tragedy*, passim.
236. *W. P.*, § 255, 258, 710, 462, 392, 305.

that proceeds from weakness. What is happiness? The feeling that power is increasing, that resistance is being overcome.[237] This is not orthodox ethics, and perhaps it will not do for long ears - though an unspoiled youth would understand it. A healthy and vigorous boy will look up sarcastically if you ask him, "Do you wish to become virtuous?" But ask him, "Do you wish to become stronger than your comrades?" and he is all eagerness at once.[238] Youth knows that ability is virtue; watch the athletic field. Youth is not at home in the classroom, because there knowledge is estranged from action; and youth measures the height of what a man knows by the depth of his power to do.[239] There is a better gospel in the boy on the field than in the man in the pulpit.

Which of the boys whom we know do we love best in our secret hearts - the prayerful Aloysius, or the masterful leader of the urchins in the street? We moralize and sermonize in mean efforts to bring the young tyrant down to our virtuous anemia; but we know that we are wrong, and respect him most when he stands his ground most firmly. To require of strength that it should express itself as weakness is just as absurd as to require of weakness that it should express itself as strength.[240] Let us go to school to our children, and we shall understand that all native propensities are beneficent, that the evil impulses are to a far view as necessary and preservative as the good.[241] In truth we worship youth because at its finest it is a free discharge of instinctive strength; and we know that happiness is nothing else than that. To abandon instinct, to deliberate, to clog action with conscious thought - that is to achieve old age. After all, nothing can be done perfectly so long as it is done consciously; consciousness is a defect to be overcome.[242] Instinct is the most intelligent of all kinds of intelligence which have hitherto been discovered.[243] Genius lies in the instincts, goodness too; all consciousness is theatricality.[244] When a people begins to worship reason, it begins to die.[245] Youth knows better: it follows instinct trustfully, and worships power.

And we worship power too, and should say so were we as honest as our children. Our gentlest virtues are but forms of power: out of the abundance of the power of sex come kindness and pity, out of revenge, justice, out of the love of resistance, bravery. Love is a secret path to the heart of the powerful; in order to become his master; gratitude is revenge of a lofty kind; self-sacrifice is an attempt to share in the power of him to

---

237. *Antich.*, § 2.
238. *W. P.*, § 918.
239. *T. O. S.*, p. 76.
240. *G. M.*, p. 45.
241. *J. W.*, § 4.
242. *Antich.*, § 14.
243. *B. G. E.*, p. 162.
244. *W. P.*, § 440, 289.
245. *E. H.*, p. 10.

whom the sacrifice is made. Honor is the acknowledgment of an equal power; praise is the pride of the judge; all conferring of benefits is an exercise of power.[246] Behold a man in distress: straightway the compassionate ones come to him, depict his misfortune to him, at last go away, satisfied and elevated; they have gloated over the unhappy man's misfortune and their own; they have spent a pleasant Sunday afternoon.[247] So with the scientist and the philosopher: in their thirst for knowledge lurks the lust of gain and conquest. And the cry of the oppressed for freedom is again a cry for power.[248]

You cannot understand man, you cannot understand society, until you learn to see in all things this will to power. Physiologists should bethink themselves before putting down the instinct of self-preservation as the cardinal instinct of an organic being. A living thing seeks above all to discharge its strength: self-preservation is only one of the results of this. And psychologists should think twice before saying that happiness or pleasure is the motive of all action. Pleasure is but an incident of the restless search for power; happiness is an accompanying, not an actuating, factor. The feeling of happiness lies precisely in the discontentedness of the will, in the fact that without opponents and obstacles it is never satisfied. Man is now master of the forces of nature, and master too of his own wild and unbridled feelings; in comparison with primitive man the man of today represents an enormous quantum of power, but not an increase of happiness. How can one maintain, then, that man has striven after happiness? No; not happiness, but more power; not peace at any price, but war; not virtue; but capacity; that is the secret of man's longing and man's seeking.[249]

Let biologists, too, re-examine the stock-in-trade of their theory. Life is not the continuous adjustment of internal to external relations, but will to power, which, proceeding from within, subjugates and incorporates an ever-increasing quantity of "external phenomena." All motive force, all "causation" whatever, is this will to power; there is no other force, physical, dynamical, or psychical.[250] As to the famous "struggle for existence," it seems at present to be more of an assumption than a fact. It does occur, but as an exception; and it is due not to a desire for food but *a tergo* to a surcharge of energy demanding discharge. The general condition of life is not one of want or famine, but rather of riches, of lavish luxuriance, and even of absurd prodigality; where there is a struggle it is a struggle for power. We must not confound Malthus with Nature.[251] One

---

246. *W. P.*, § 255, 774, 775; *D. D.*, § 215; *J. W.*, § 13.
247. *D. D.*, § 224.
248. *W. P.*, § 376, 776.
249. *W. P.*, § 650, 657, 685, 696, 704; *Antich.*, § 2.
250. *Ibid.*, § 681, 688, 689.
251. *T. I.* p. 71; *W. P.*, § 649.

does indeed find the "cruelty of Nature" which is so often referred to, but in a different place: Nature is cruel, but against her lucky and well-constituted children; she protects and shelters and loves the lowly. Darwin sees selection in favor of the stronger, the better constituted. Precisely the reverse stares one in the face: the suppression of the lucky cases, the reversion to average, the uselessness of the more highly constituted types, the inevitable mastery of the mediocre. If we drew our morals from reality, they would read thus: the mediocre are more valuable than the exceptional creatures; the will to nonentity prevails over the will to life. We have to beware of this formulation of reality into a moral.[252]

No; morality is not mediocrity, it is superiority; it does not mean being like most people, but being better, stronger, more capable than most people. It does not mean timidity: if anything is virtue it is to stand unafraid in the presence of any prohibition.[253] It does not mean the pursuit of ends sanctified by society; it means the will to your own ends, and to the means to them. It means behaving as states behave - with frank abandonment of all altruistic pretence. Corporate bodies are intended to do that which individuals have not the courage to do: for this reason all communities are vastly more upright and instructive as regards the nature of man than individuals, who are too cowardly to have the courage of their desires. All altruism is the prudence of the private man; societies are not mutually altruistic. Altruism and life are incompatible: all the forces and instincts which are the source of life lie stagnant beneath the ban of the old morality. But real morality is certainty of instinct, effectiveness of action; it is any action which increases the power of a man or of men; it is an expression of ascendant and expanding life; it is achievement; it is power.[254]

The Superman

With such a morality you breed men who are men, and to breed men who are men is all that your "social problem" comes to. This does not mean that the whole race is to be improved: the very last thing a sensible man would promise to accomplish would be to improve mankind. Mankind does not improve, it does not even exist. The aspect of the whole is much more like that of a huge experimenting workshop where some things in all ages succeed, while an incalculable number of things fail. To say that the social problem consists in a general raising of the average standard of comfort and ability amounts to abandoning the problem; there is as little prospect of mankind's attaining to a higher order as there is for the ant and the ear-wig to enter into kinship with God and eter-

252. W. P., § 685.
253. Z., p. 398.
254. W. P., § 880, 716, 343, 423, 291.

nity. The most fundamental of all errors here lies in regarding the many, the herd, as an aim instead of the individual: the herd is only a means. The road to perfection lies in the bringing forth of the most powerful individuals, for whose use the great masses would be converted into mere tools, into the most intelligent and flexible tools possible. Every human being, with his total activity, has dignity and significance only so far as he is, consciously or unconsciously, a tool in the service of a superior individual. All that can be done is to produce here and there, now and then, such a superior individual, *l'uomo singulare*, the higher man, the superman. The problem does not concern what humanity as a whole or as a species is to accomplish, but what kind of man is to be desired as highest in value, what kind of man is to be worked for and bred. To produce the superman: that is the social problem. If this is not understood, nothing is understood.[255]

Now what would such a man be like? Shall we try to picture him?

We see him as above all a lover of life: strong enough, too, to love life without deceiving himself about it. There is no *memento mori* here; rather a *memento vivere*; rich instincts call for much living. A hard man, loving danger and difficulty: what does not kill him, he feels, leaves him stronger. Pleasure - pleasure as it is understood by the rich - is repugnant to him: he seeks not pleasure but work, not happiness but responsibility and achievement. He does not make philosophy an excuse for living prudently and apart, an artifice for withdrawing successfully from the game of life; he does not stand aside and merely look on; he puts his shoulder to the wheel; for him it is the essence of philosophy to feel the obligation and burden of a hundred attempts and temptations, the joy of a hundred adventures; he risks himself constantly; he plays out to the end this bad game.[256]

To risk and to create, this is the meaning of life to the superman. He could not bear to be a man, if man could not be a poet, a maker. To change every "It was" into a "Thus I would have it!" - in this he finds that life may redeem itself. He is moved not by ambition but by a mighty overflowing spendthrift spirit that drives him on; he must remake; for this he compels all things to come to him and into him, in order that they may flow back from him as gifts of his love and his abundance; in this refashioning of things by thought he sees the holiness of life; the greatest events, he knows, are these still creative hours.[257]

He is a man of contrasts, or contradictions; he does not desire to be always the same man; he is a multitude of elements and of men; his value lies precisely in his comprehensiveness and multi-fariousness, in the variety of burdens which he can bear, in the extent to which he can stretch

255. *E. H.*, p. 2; *D. D.*, § 49; *Lonely N.*, p. 17; *W. P.*, § 269, 90, 766, 660.
256. *E. H.*, p. 138; *T. O. S.*, II, p. 66; *Z.*, p. 222; *W. P.*, p. 934, 944; *J. W.*, p. 8; *T. I.*, 40; *B. G. E.*, p.I38.
257. *Z.*, p. 199, 103, 186; *W. P.*, § 792.

his responsibility; in him the antagonistic character of existence is repre-
sented and justified. He loves instinct, knows that it is the fountain of all
his energies; but he knows, too, the natural delight of aesthetic natures in
measure, the pleasure of self-restraint, the exhilaration of the rider on a
fiery steed. He is a selective principle, he rejects much; he reacts slowly
to all kinds of stimuli, with that tardiness which long caution and deliberate pride have bred in him; he tests the approaching stimulus. He decides
slowly; but he holds firmly to a decision made.[258]

He loves and has the qualities which the folk call virtues, but he loves
too and shows the qualities which the folk call vices; it is again in this
union of opposites that he rises above mediocrity; he is a broad arch that
spans two banks lying far apart. The folk on either side fear him, for they
cannot calculate on him, or classify him. He is a free spirit, an enemy of
all fetters and labels; he belongs to no party, knowing that the man who
belongs to a party perforce becomes a liar. He is a skeptic (not that he
must appear to be one); freedom from any kind of conviction is a necessary factor in his strength of will. He does not make propaganda or pros-
elytes; he keeps his ideals to himself as distinctions: his opinion is *his*
opinion: another person has not easily a right to it; he has renounced the
bad taste of wishing to agree with many people. He knows that he cannot reveal himself to anybody; like everything profound, he loves the
mask; he does not descend to familiarity; and is not familiar when people
think he is. If he cannot lead, he walks alone.[259]

He has not only intellect; if that were all it would not be enough; he
has blood. Behind him is a lineage of culture and ability; lives of danger
and distinction; his ancestors have paid the price for what he is, just as
most men pay the price for what their ancestors have been. Naturally,
then, he has a strong feeling of distance; he sees inequality and grada-
tion, order and rank, everywhere among men. He has the most aristocratic of virtues: intellectual honesty. He does not readily become a friend
or an enemy; he honors only his equals, and therefore cannot be the
enemy of many; where one despises one cannot wage war. He lacks the
power of easy reconciliation; but "retaliation" is as incomprehensible to
him as "equal rights." He remains just even as regards his injurer; despite
the strong provocation of personal insult the clear and lofty objectivity of
the just and judging eye (whose glance is as profound as it is gentle) is
untroubled. He recognizes duties only to his equals; to others he does
what he thinks best; he knows that justice is found only among equals.
He has that distinctively aristocratic trait, the ability to command and with
equal readiness to obey; that is indispensable to his pride. He will not permit himself to be praised; he does what serves his purpose. The essence
of him is that he has a purpose, for which he will not hesitate to run all

258. *W. P.*, § 881, 870, 918; *B. G. E.*, p., 154; *E. H.*, p. 13; *D. D.*, § 562.
259. *W. P.*, § 967, 366-7, 349; *Z.*, p. 141; *Antich.*, § 55;. *B. G. E.*, pp. 54, 57.

risks, even to sacrifice men, to bend their backs to the worst. That something may exist which is a hundred times more important than the question whether he feels well or unwell, and therefore too whether the others feel well or unwell: this is a fundamental instinct of his nature. To have a purpose, and to cleave to it through all dangers till it be achieved - that is his great passion, that is himself.[260]

How to Make Supermen

It is our task, then, to procreate this synthetic man, who embodies everything and justifies it, and for whom the rest of mankind is but soil; to bring the philosopher, the artist, and the saint, within and without us, to the light, and to strive thereby for the completion of nature. In this cultivation lies the meaning of culture: the direction of all life to the end of producing the finest possible individuals. What is great in man is that he is a bridge and not a goal; his very essence is to create a being higher than himself; that is the instinct of procreation, the instinct of action and of work. Even the higher man himself feels this need of begetting; and for lesser men all virtue and morals lie in preparing the way that the superman may come. There is no greater horror than the degenerating soul which says, "All for myself." In this great purpose, too, is the essence of a better religion, and a surpassing of the bounds of narrow individualism; with this purpose there come moments, sparks from the clear fire of love, in whose light we understand the word "I" no longer; we feel that we are creating, and therefore in a sense becoming, something greater than ourselves.[261]

How to make straight the way for the superman? First by reforming marriage. Let it be understood at once that love is a hindrance rather than a help to such marriages as are calculated to breed higher men. To regard a thing as beautiful is necessarily to regard it falsely; that is why love marriages are from the social point of view the most unreasonable form of matrimony. Were there a benevolent God, the marriages of men would cause him more displeasure than anything else; he would observe that all buyers are careful, but that even the most cunning one buys his wife in a sack, and surely he would cause the earth to tremble in convulsions when a saint and a goose couple. When a man is in love, he should not be allowed to come to a decision about his life, and to determine once for all the character of his lifelong society on account of a whim. If we treated marriage seriously, we would publicly declare invalid the vows of lovers, and refuse them permission to marry.[262] We would remake pub-

---

260. *W. P.*, § 969. 371, 356, 926, 946, 26; *Z.*, p. 430; *E. H.*, pp. 23, 19, 128; *G. M.*, p. 85; *D. D.*, § 60.
261. *W. P.*, § 866; *T. O. S.*, II, p. 154; *Z.*, pp.8, 104; *T. I.*, p.269.
262. Under Nietzsche's guidelines, Will Durant would never have been allowed to marry his beloved Ariel. Not simply because of the impulsiveness of his actions (she was young and one of his students), but also

lic opinion, so that it would encourage trial marriage; we would exact certificates of health and good ancestry; we would punish bachelorhood by longer military service, and would reward with all sorts of privileges those fathers who should lavish sons upon the world. And above all we would make people understand that the purpose of marriage is not that they should duplicate, but that they should surpass, themselves. Perhaps we would read to them from *Zarathustra*, with fitting ceremonies and solemnities: "Thou art young, and wishest for child and marriage. But I ask thee, art thou a man who dareth to wish for a child? Art thou the victorious one, the self-subduer, the commander of thy senses, the master of thy virtues? Or in thy wish doth there speak the animal, or necessity? Or solitude? Or discord with thyself? I would that thy victory and freedom were longing for a child. Thou shalt build living monuments unto thy victory and thy liberation. Thou shalt build beyond thyself. But first thou must build thyself square in body and soul. Thou shalt not only propagate thyself, but propagate thyself upward! Marriage: thus I call the will of two to create that one which is more than they who created it. I call marriage reverence unto each other as unto those who will such a will."[263]

In a word, eugenic marriage; and after eugenic marriage, rigorous education. But interest in education will become powerful only when belief in a God and his care have been abandoned, just as medicine began to flourish only when the belief in miraculous cures had lapsed. When men begin at last to *believe* in education, they will endure much rather than have their sons miss going to a good and hard school at the proper time. What is it that one learns in a hard school? To obey and to command. For this is what distinguishes hard schooling, as good schooling, from every other schooling, namely that a good deal is demanded, severely exacted; that excellence is required as if it were normal; that praise is scanty, that leniency is non-existent; that blame is sharp, practical, and without reprieve, and has no regard to talent and antecedents. To prefer danger to comfort; not to weigh in a tradesman's balance what is permitted and what is forbidden; to be more hostile to pettiness, slyness, and parasitism than to wickedness - we are in every need of a school where these things would be taught. Such a school would allow its pupils to learn productively, by living and doing; it would not subject them to the tyranny of books and the weight of the past; it would teach them less about the past and more about the future; it would teach them the future of humanity as depending on human, will, on their will; it would prepare the way for and be a part of a vast enterprise in breeding and education.[264] But even such a school would not provide all that is necessary

---

because she was a poor Russian Jew who likely would not have passed Nietzsche's certification standards for "health and good ancestry".
263. *W. P.*, § 804, 732-3; *Z.*, pp. 94-6; *D. D.*, § 150-1.
264. *H. H.*, § 242; *W. P.*, § 912; *B. G. E.*, p. 129; *D. D.*, § 194; "Schopenhaur" (in *T.O.S.*), passim.

in education. Not all should receive the same training and the same care; select groups must be chosen, and special instruction lavished on them; the greatest success, however, will remain for the man who does not seek to educate either everybody or certain limited circles, but only one single individual. The last century was superior to ours precisely because it possessed so many individually educated men.

On the Necessity of Exploitation

And next slavery.

This is one of those ugly words which are the *verba non grata* of modern discussion, because they jar us so ruthlessly out of the grooves of our thinking. Nevertheless it is clear to all but those to whom self-deception is the staff of life that as the honest Greeks had it, some are born to be slaves. Try to educate all men equally, and you become the laughing-stock of your own maturity. The masses seem to be worth notice in three aspects only: first as the copies of great men, printed on bad paper from worn-out plates; next as a contrast to the great men; and lastly as their tools. Living consists in living at the cost of others: the man who has not grasped this fact has not taken the first step towards truth to himself. And to consider distress of all kinds as an objection, as something which must be done away with, is the greatest nonsense on earth; almost as mad as the will to abolish bad weather, out of pity to the poor, so to speak. The masses must be used, whether that means or does not mean that they must suffer; - it requires great strength to live and forget how far life and injustice are one. What is the suffering of whole peoples compared to the creative agonies of great individuals?[265]

There are many who threw away everything they were worth when they threw away their slavery. In all respects slaves live more securely and more happily than modern laborers; the laborer chooses his harder lot to satisfy the vanity of telling himself that he is not a slave. These men are dangerous; not because they are strong, but because they are sick; it is the sick who are the greatest danger to the healthy; it is the weak ones, they who mouth so much about their sickness, who vomit bile and call it newspaper - it is they who instill the most dangerous venom and skepticism into our trust in life, in man, and in ourselves; it is they who most undermine the life beneath our feet. It is for such as these that Christianity may serve a good purpose (so serving our purpose too). Those qualities which are within the grasp only of the strongest and most terrible natures, and which make their existence possible - leisure, adventure, disbelief, and even dissipation - would necessarily ruin mediocre natures - and does do so when they possess them. In the case of the lat-

---

265. *T. O. S.*, II. pp. 84, 28; *W. P.*, § 369, 965; *E. H.*, p. 135.

ter, industry, regularity, moderation, and strong "conviction" are in their proper place - in short, all "gregarious virtues"; under their influence these mediocre men become perfect. We good Europeans, then, though atheists and immoralists, will take care to support the religions and the morality which are associated with the gregarious instinct; for by means of them an order of men is, so to speak, prepared, which must at some time or other fall into our hands, which must actually crave for our hands.[266]

Slavery, let us understand it well, is the necessary price of culture; the free work, or art, of some involves the compulsory labor of others. As in the organism so in society: the higher function is possible only through the subjection of the lower functions. A high civilization is a pyramid; it can stand only on a broad base, its first prerequisite is a strongly and soundly consolidated mediocrity. In order that there may be a broad, deep, and fruitful soil for the development of art, the enormous majority must, in the service of a minority, be slavishly subjected. At their cost, through the surplus of their labor, that privileged class is to be relieved from the struggle for existence, in order to create and to satisfy a new world of want. The misery of the toilers must still increase in order to make the production of a world of art possible to a small number of Olympian men.[267]

Aristocracy

The greatest folly of the strong is to let the weak make them ashamed to exploit, to let the weak suggest to them, "It is a shame to be happy - there is too much misery!" Let us therefore reaffirm the right of the happy to existence, the right of bells with a full tone over bells that are cracked and discordant. Not that exploitation as such is desirable; it is good only where it supports and develops an aristocracy of higher men who are themselves developing still higher men. This philosophy aims not at an individualistic morality but at a new order of rank. In this age of universal suffrage, in this age in which everybody is allowed to sit in judgment upon everything and everybody, one feels compelled to reestablish the order of rank. The higher men must be protected from contamination and suffocation by the lower. The richest and most complex forms perish so easily! Only the lowest succeed in maintaining their apparent imperishableness.[268]

The first question as to the order of rank: how far is a man disposed to be solitary or gregarious? If he is disposed to be gregarious, his value consists in those qualities which secure the survival of his tribe or type; if he is disposed to be solitary, his qualities are those which distinguish him from others; hence the important consequence: the solitary type should

266. *Z*; pp. 84, 64; *H. H.*, § 457; *G. M.*, 156-7; *B. G. E.*, 61-2; *W. P.*, § 373, 901, 132.
267. *H. H.*, § 439: *W. P.*, § 660: *Antich.*, § 57; *Lonely N.*, p.7.
268. *G. M.*, pp. 160-1; *W. P.*, § 287, 854, 864.

not be valued from the standpoint of the gregarious type, or *vice versa*. Viewed from above, both types are necessary; and so is their antago- nism. Degeneration lies in the approximation of the qualities of the herd to those of the solitary creature, and *vice versa*; in short, in their begin- ning to resemble each other. Hence the difference in their virtues, their rights and their obligations; in the light of this difference one comes to abhor the vulgarity of Stuart Mill when he says, "What is right for one man is right for another." It is not; what is right for the herd is precisely what is wrong for their leaders; and what is right for the leaders is wrong for the herd. The leaders use, the herd is used; the virtues of either lie in the effi- ciency here of leadership, there of service. Slave-morality is one thing, and master-morality another.[269]

And leadership of course requires an aristocracy. Let us repeat it: democracy has always been the death-agony of the power of organiza- tion and direction; these require great aristocratic families, with long tra- ditions of administration and leadership; old ancestral lines that guaran- tee for many generations the duration of the necessary will and the nec- essary instincts. Not only aristocracy, then, but caste; for if a man have plebeian ancestors, his soul will be a plebeian soul; education, discipline, culture will be wasted on him, merely enabling him to become a great liar. Therefore intermarriage, even social intercourse of leaders with herd, is to be avoided with all precaution and intolerance; too much intercourse with barbarians ruined the Romans, and will ruin any noble race.[270]

In what direction may one turn with any hope of finding even the aspi- ration for such an aristocracy? Only there where a *noble* attitude of mind prevails, an attitude of mind which believes in slavery and in manifold orders of rank, as the prerequisites of any higher degree of culture. Men with this attitude of mind will insistently call for, and will at last produce, philosophical men of power, artist-tyrants - a higher kind of men which, thanks to their preponderance of will, knowledge, riches, and influence, will avail themselves of democratic Europe as the most suitable and sub- tle instrument for taking the fate of Europe into their hands, and working as artists upon man himself. The fundamental belief of these great desir- ers will be that society must not be allowed to exist for its own sake, but only as the foundation and scaffolding by means of which a select class of beings may be able to elevate themselves to their highest duties, and in general to a higher existence: like those sun-climbing plants in Java which encircle an oak so long and so often with their arms that at last, high above it, but supported by it, they can unfold their tops in the open light, and exhibit their happiness.[271]

269. *W. P.*, § 886, 926.
270. *W. P.*, § 886, 926.
271. *W. P.*, § 464, 960; *B. G. E.*, p. 225.

Signs of Ascent

Are we moving toward such a consummation?

Can we detect about us any signs of this ascending movement of life? Not signs of "progress"; that is another narcotic, like Christianity - good for slaves, but to be avoided by those who rule. Man as a species is not progressing; the general level of the species is not raised. But humanity as mass sacrificed to the prosperity of the one stronger type of Man - that *would be* a progress.[272]

Progress of this kind, to some degree, there has always been. The ruling class in Greece, as seen in Homer and even in Thucydides (though with Socrates degeneration begins), is an example of this kind of progress or attainment. Imagine this culture, which has its poet in Sophocles, its statesman in Pericles, its physician in Hippocrates, its natural philosopher in Democritus; here is a yea-saying, a gratitude, to life in all its manifestations; here life is understood, and covered with art that it may be borne; here men are frivolous so that they may forget for a moment the arduousness and perilousness of their task; they are superficial, but from profundity; they exalt philosophers who preach moderation, because they themselves are so immoderate, so instinctive, so hilariously wild; they are great, they are elevated above any ruling class before or after them because here the morals of the governing caste have grown up among the governing caste, and not among the herd.[273]

We catch some of the glory of these Greeks in the men of the Renaissance: men perfect in their immorality, terrible in their demands; we should not dare to stand amid the conditions which produced these men and which these men produced; we should not even dare to imagine ourselves in those conditions: our nerves would not endure that reality - not to speak of our muscles. One man of their type, continuator and development of their type, brother (as Taine most rightly says) of Dante and Michelangelo, one such man we have known with less of the protection of distance; and he was too hard to bear. That *Ens Realissimum*, synthesis of monster and superman, surnamed Napoleon! The first man, and the man of greatest initiative and developed views, of modern times; a man of tolerance, not out of weakness, but out of strength, able to risk the full enjoyment of naturalness and be strong enough for this freedom. In such a man we see something in the nature of "disinterestedness" in his work on his marble, whatever be the number of men that are sacrificed in the process. Men were glad to serve him; as most normal men are glad to serve the great man; the crowd was tired of "equal rights," tired of being masterless; it longed to worship genius again. What was the excuse for that terrible farce, the French Revolution? It made men ready for

272. *W. P.*, § 44, 684, 909; *G. M.*, p. 91.
273. *D. D.*, § 165, 168; *W. P.*, § 1052; *B. G. E.*, p. 69; *J. W.*, p. 10.

Napoleon.[274]

When shall we produce another superman? Let us go back to our question: Can we detect about us any signs of strength?

Yes. We are learning to get along without God. We are recovering from the noble sentiments of Rousseau. We are giving the body its due; physiology is overcoming theology. We are lees hungry for lies - we are facing squarely some of the ugliness of life - prostitution, for example. We speak less of "duty" and "principles"; we are not so enamored of bourgeois conventions. We are less ashamed of our instincts; we no longer believe in a right which proceeds from a power that is unable to uphold it. There is an advance towards "naturalness": in all political questions, even in the relations between parties, even in merchants', workmen's circles only questions of power come into play; what one can do is the first question, what one ought to do is a secondary consideration. There is a certain degree of liberal-mindedness regarding morality; where this is most distinctly wanting we regard its absence as a sign of a morbid condition (Carlyle, Ibsen, Schopenhauer); if there is anything which can reconcile us to our age it is precisely the amount of immorality which it allows itself without falling in its own estimation.[275]

Modern science, despite its narrowing specialization, is a sign of ascent. Here is strictness in service, inexorability in small matters as well as great, rapidity in weighing, judging, and condemning; the hardest is demanded here, the best is done without reward of praise or distinction; it is rather as among soldiers - almost nothing but blame and sharp reprimand is heard; for doing well prevails here as the rule, and the rule has, as everywhere, a silent tongue. It is the same with this "severity of science" as with the manners and politeness of the best society: it frightens the uninitiated. He, however, who is accustomed to it, does not like to live anywhere but in this clear, transparent, powerful, and highly electrified atmosphere, this *manly* atmosphere.[276]

In this achievement of science lies such au opportunity as philosophy has never had before. Science traces the course of things but points to no goal: what it does give consists of the fundamental facts upon which the new goal must be based. All the sciences have now to pave the way for the future task of the philosopher; this task being understood to mean that he must solve the problem of *value*, that he has to fix the hierarchy of values. He must become lawgiver, commander; he must determine the "whither" and "why" for mankind. All knowledge must be at his disposal, and must serve him as a tool for creation.[277]

Most certain of the signs of a reascending movement of life is the

274. *T. I.*, p. 91, 110; *J. W.*, § 362; *G. M.*, pp. 56, 225; *W. P.*, § 975, 877; *B. G. E.*, pp. 201, 53.
275. *W. P.*, § 109-34, 747.
276. *J. W.*; § 293.
277. *T. I.*, p. 260; *G. M.*, p. 58; *B. G. E.*, p. 151; *Lonely N.*, p. 221.

development of militarism. The military development of Europe is a delightful surprise. This fine discipline is teaching us to do our duty without expecting praise. Universal military service is the curious antidote which we possess for the effeminacy of democratic ideas. Men are learning again the joy of living in danger. Some of them are even learning the old truth that war is good in itself, aside from any gain in land or other wealth; instead of saying "A good cause will hallow every war," they learn to say "A good war hallows every cause." When the instincts of a society ultimately make it give up war and conquest, it is decadent: it is ripe for democracy and the rule of shopkeepers. A state which should prevent war would not only be committing suicide (for war is just as necessary to the state as the slave is to society); it would be hostile to life, it would be an outrage on the future of man. The maintenance of the military state is the last means of adhering to the great traditions of the past; or where it has been lost, of reviving it. Only in this can the superior or strong type of man be preserved.[278]

A nation is a detour of nature to arrive at six or seven great men, and then to get around them. The state is the organization of immorality for the attainment of this purpose. But as existing today, the state is a very imperfect instrument, subject at any moment to democratic foundering. What concerns the thinker here is the slow and hesitant formation of a united Europe. This was the thought, and the sole real work and impulse, of the only broad-minded and deep-thinking men of this century - the tentative effort to anticipate the future of "the European." Only in their weaker moments, or when they grew old, did they fall back again into the national narrowness of the "Fatherlanders" - then they were once more "patriots." One thinks here of men like Napoleon, Heine, Goethe, Beethoven, Stendhal, Schopenhauer. And after all, is there a single idea behind this bovine nationalism? What possible value can there be in encouraging this arrogant self-conceit when everything today points to greater and more common interests? At a moment when the spiritual dependence and denationalization which are obvious to all are paving the way for the *rapprochements* and fertilizations which make up the real value and sense of present-day culture?[279]

What an instrument such a united Europe would be for the development, and protection and expression of superior individuals! What a buoyant ascent of life after this long descent into democracy! See now, in review, the two movements which we have studied and on which we have strung our philosophy: on the one hand Christian mythology and morality, the cult of weakness, the fear of life, the deterioration of the species, ever increasing suppression of the privileged and the strong, the lapse into democracy, feminism, socialism, and at last into anarchy, all termi-

278. *W. P.*, § 127, 728-9; *G. M.*, pp. 88, 226; *J. W.*, § 283; *Z.*, p. 60; *Lonely N.* p. 15.
279. *B. G. E.*, p. 94; *W. P.*, § 717, 748; *G. M.*, pp. 223-4.

nating in pessimism, despair, total loss of the love of life; on the other hand the reaffirmation of the worth of life, the resolute distinction between slave-morality and master-morality, the recognition of the aristocratic valuation of health, vigor, energy, as moral in all their forms, and of the will to power as the source and significance of all action and all living; the conception of the higher man, of the exceptional individual, as the goal of human endeavor; the redirection of marriage, of education, of social structure, to the fostering and cherishing of these higher types; culminating in the supernational organization of Europe as the instrumentality and artistic expression of the superior man.[280]

Is this philosophy too hard to bear? Very well. But those races that cannot bear it are doomed; and those which regard it as the greatest blessing are destined to be masters of the world.[281]

END EXPOSI(TION[282]

Criticism

What shall one say to this? What would a democrat say - such a democrat as would be a friend to socialism and feminism, and even to anarchism - and a lover of Jesus? One pictures such a man listening with irritated patience to the foregoing, and responding very readily to an invitation to take the floor.

There are lessons here, he begins, as if brushing away an initial encumbrance. There is something of Nietzsche in all of us, just as there is something of Jesus (almost as there is something of man and of woman in all of us, as Weininger argued), and part of that crowd called *myself* is flattered by this doctrine of ruthless power. Nietzsche stood outside our social and moral structure, he was a sort of hermit in the world of thought, and so he could see things in that structure which are too near to our noses for easy vision. And as you listen to him you see history anew as a long succession of masterings and enslavings and deceivings, and you become almost reconciled to the future being nothing but a further succession of the same. And then you begin to see that if the future is to be different, one of the things we must do is to pinch ourselves out of this Nietzschean dream.[283]

And a good way to begin is with Nietzsche's own principle, that every philosophy is a physiology.[284] He asks us to believe that there is no such

---

280. *W. P.*, § 712.
281. *Ibid.*, § 1053.
282. Here Durant returns to his own voice and begins his critique of Nietzsche's philosophy.
283. Extremely prescient of Durant at this point, as he has fairly predicted the abuse of Nietzsche's philosophy by the Third Reich under Hitler.
284. *J. W.*, p. 5.

thing as a morbid trait in him,[285] "but we must not take him at his word. The most important point about this philosophy is that it was written by a sick man, a man sick to the very roots - if you will let me say it, abnormal in sexual constitution - a man not sufficiently attracted to the other sex, because he has so much of the other sex in him. "She is a woman," he writes in *Zarathustra*, "and never loves anyone but a warrior"; that is, if Nietzsche but knew it, the diagnosis of his own disease. This hatred of women, this longing for power, this admiration for strength, for successful lying,[286] this inability to see a *tertium quid* between tyranny and slavery[287] - all these are feminine traits. A stronger man would not have been so shrewishly shrill about woman and Christianity; a stronger man would have needed less repetition, less emphasis and underlining, less of italics and exclamation points; a stronger man would have been more gentle, and would have smiled where Nietzsche scolds. It is the philosophy, you see, of a man abnormally weak in the social instincts, and at the same time lacking in proper outlet for such social instincts as nature has left him.

Consequently, he never gets beyond the individual. He thinks society is made up of individuals, when it is really made up of groups. He supposes that the only virtues a man can have are those which help him as an isolated unit; the idea that a man may find self-expression in social expression, in cooperation, that there are virtues which are virtues because they enable one to work with others against a common evil - this notion never occurs to him. He does not see that sympathy and mutual aid, for example, though they preserve some inferior individuals, yet secure that group-solidarity, and therefore group-survival, without which even the strong ones would perish.[288] He does not imagine that perhaps the barbarians who invaded Rome needed the gospel of a, "gentle Jesus meek and mild" if anything at all was to remain of that same classical culture which he paints so lovingly.[289] He laughs at self-denial; and then invites you to devote yourself forever to some self-elected superman.

This philosophy of aristocracy, of the necessity of slavery, of the absurdity of democracy - of course it is exciting to all weak people who would like to have power - and who have not read it all before in Plato. In this particular case the humor of the situation lies in the very powerful attack which Nietzsche makes on the irreligious religious humbug which has proved one of the chief instruments of mastery in the hands of the class whose power he is trying to strengthen. "I hope to be forgiven," says

---

285. *E. H.*, p. 53.
286. *W. P.*, § 544, with footnote Quoting Napoleon: "An almost instinctive belief with me is that all strong men lie when they speak, and much more so when they write."
287. "Far too long a slave and a tyrant have been hidden in woman; she is not yet capable of friendship." - *Z.*, p.75.
288. Hobhouse, *Social Evolution and Political Theory*, New York, 1911, p. 25.
289. There is something verging: on recognition of this in *W. P.*, 403-4.

Nietzsche, "for discovering that all moral philosophy hitherto has belonged to the soporific appliances."[290] "Discovering" as if the aristocracy had not known that all along! "Here is a naive bookworm," these "strong men" will say among themselves, "who has discovered what every one of us knows. He presumes to tell us how to increase our power, and he can find no better way of helping us than to expose in print the best secrets of our trade."

Just in this lies the value of Nietzsche, as Rousseau said of Machiavelli: he lets us in behind the scenes of the drama of exploitation. We know better now the men with whom democracy must deal. We see the greed for power that hides behind the contention that culture cannot exist without slavery. Grant that contention: so much the worse for culture! If culture means the increasing concentration of the satisfactions of life in the hands of a few "superior" pigs, their culture may be dispensed with; if it is to stay, it will have to mean the direction of knowledge and ability to the spread of the satisfactions of life. Which is finer - the relationship of master and slave, or that of friend and friend? Surely a world of people liking and helping one another is a finer world to live in than one in which the instincts of aggression are supreme. And such a cooperative civilization need not fear the tests of survival; selection puts an ever higher premium on solidarity, an ever lower value on pugnacity. Intelligence, not ready anger, will win the great contests of the future. Friendship will pay.[291]

The history of the world is a record of the patient and planful attempt to replace hatred by understanding, narrowness by large vision, opposition by cooperation, slavery by friendship. Friendship. a word to be avoided by those who would appear *blasé*. But let us repeat it; words have been known to nourish deeds which without them might never have grown into reality. Some find heaven in making as many men as possible their slaves; others find heaven in making as many men as possible their friends. Which type of man will we have? Which type of man, if abundant, would make this world a splendor and a delight?

The hope for which Jesus lived was that man might some day come to mean friend. It is the only hope worth living for.

Nietzsche Replies

"It is certainly not the least charm of a theory," says Nietzsche, "that

---

290. *B. G. E.*, p. 173.
291. And here Durant demonstrates shades of his ardent socialism. Like many dreamers of his intellectual class at the turn of the 20th century, Will Durant believed that socialism would remake the world into a better place. It was not until he journeyed to communist Russia in the 1930s that Durant realized the inherent failures of the socialist philosophy, at which point he wrote his book, *The Tragedy of Russia*. While he remained consistently a democrat for the remainder of his life, his experience in Russia forever changed his view on pure socialism.

it is refutable."[292]   But "what have I to do with mere refutations?"[293] "A prelude I am of better players."[294] "Verily, I counsel you," said Zarathustra, "depart from me and defend yourselves against Zarathustra! And better still, be ashamed of him. Perhaps he hath deceived you. The man of perception must not only be able to love his enemies, but also to hate his friends. One ill requiteth one's teacher by always remaining only his scholar. Why will ye not pluck at my wreath? Ye revere me; but how if your reverence one day falleth down? Beware of being crushed to death with a statue! Ye say ye believe in Zarathustra? But what is Zarathustra worth? Ye are my faithful ones; but what are all faithful ones worth? When ye had not yet sought yourselves ye found me. Thus do all faithful ones; hence all belief is worth so little. Now I ask you to lose me and find yourselves; not until all of you have disowned me shall I return unto you."[295]

Conclusion

"Look," says Rudin, in Turgenev's story, "you see that apple tree? It has broken down with the weight and multitude of its own fruit. It is the emblem of genius." "To perish beneath a load one can neither bear nor throw off," wrote Nietzsche, "that is a philosopher."[296] I shall announce the song of the lightning, said Zarathustra, and perish in the announcing.[297]

Insanity with such a man is but a matter of time; he feels it coming upon him; he values his hours like a man condemned to execution. In twenty days he writes the *Genealogy of Morals*; in one year (1888) he produces *The Twilight of the Idols, Antichrist, The Case of Wagner, Ecce Homo,* and his longest and greatest book, *The Will to Power.* He not only writes these books; he reads the proof-sheets, straining his eyes beyond repair. He is almost blind now; he is deceived, taken advantage of, because he can hardly see farther than his touch. "If I were blind," he writes pitifully, "I should be healthy."[298] Yet his body is racked with pain: "On 118 days this year I have had severe attacks."[299] "I have given a name to my pain, and call it 'a dog' - it is just as pitiful, just as importunate and shameless; and I can domineer over it, vent my bad humor on it, as others do with their dogs, servants, and wives."[300]

Meanwhile the world lives on unnoticing, or noticing only to misun-

292. *B. G. E.*, p. 25.
293. *G. M.*, p. 6.
294. *Z.*, p. 303.
295. *Z.*, p. 107.
296. *T. I.*, p. 2.
297. *Z.*, p. 10.
298. *J. W.*, § 312.
299. *Ibid.*, p. 69, referring to 1879.
300. *Ibid.*, § 312.

derstand. "My foes have become mighty, and have so distorted my teaching, that my best beloved must be ashamed of the gifts that I gave them."[301] He learns that the libertines of Europe are using his philosophy as a cloak for their sins: "I can read in their faces that they totally misunderstand me, and that it is only the animal in them which rejoices at being able to cast off its fetters."[302] He finds one whom he thinks to make his disciple; he is buoyed up for a few days by the hope; the hope is shattered, and loneliness closes in once more upon him. "A kingdom for a kind word!" he cries out in the depth of his longing; and again he writes, "For years no milk of human kindness, no breath of love."[303]

In December, 1888, one whom he has thought friendly writes that his brother-in-law is sending to a magazine an attack on him. It is the last blow; it means that his sister has joined the others in deserting him. "I take one sleeping-draught after another to deaden the pain, but for all that I cannot sleep. Today I will take such a dose that I will lose my wits."[304] He has been taking chloral, and worse drugs, to pay for the boon of sleep; the poison tips the scale already made heavy by his blindness and eyestrain, by his loneliness, by the treachery of his friends, by his general bodily ailments; he wakes up from this final draught in a stupor from which he never recovers; he writes to Brandes and signs himself "The Crucified"; he wanders into the street, is tormented by children, falls in a fit; his good landlord helps him back to his room, sends for the simple, ignorant doctor of the neighborhood; but it is too late; the man is insane. Age, 44; another - the only name greater than his among modern philosophers - had died at that pitifully early age.

The body lingered eleven years behind the mind.

Death came in 1900. He was buried as he had wished: "Promise me," he had asked his sister, many years before, "that when I die only my friends shall stand about my coffin, and no inquisitive crowd. See that no priest or anyone else utters falsehoods at my graveside, when I can no longer defend myself; and let me descend into my tomb as an honest pagan."[305]

After his death the world began to read him. As in so many cases the life had to be given that the doctrine might be heard. "Only where there are graves," he had written in Zarathustra, "are there resurrections."[306]

---

301. *Lonely N.*, p. 206.
302. *Ibid.*, p. 218.
303. *Lonely N.*, p. 289.
304. *Ibid.*, p. 391.
305. *Ibid.*, p. 65.
306. *Ibid.*, p. 167.

PART TWO: SUGGESTIONS

CHAPTER SIX
SOLUTIONS AND DISSOLUTIONS

The Problem

And so we come through our five episodes in the history of the reconstructive mind, and find ourselves in the bewildering present, comfortably seated, let us say, in the great reading room of our Columbia Library. An attendant liberates us from the maze of "Nietzsche's Works" lying about us, and returns presently with a stack of thirty books purporting to give the latest developments in the field of social study and research. We are soon lost in their graphs and statistics, their records and results; gradually we come to feel beneath these dead facts the lives they would reveal; and as we read we see a picture.

It is the picture of one life. We see it beginning helplessly in the arms of the factory physician; it is only after some violence that it consents to breathe - as if it hesitates to enter upon its adventure. It has a touch of consumption but is otherwise a fair enough baby, says the factory physician. It will do - not saying for what or whom. Luckily, it is a boy, and will be able to work soon. He does; at the age of nine he becomes a newsboy; he is up at five in the morning and peddles news till eight; at nine he gets to school, fagged out but restless; he gives trouble; cannot memorize quickly enough, nor sit still long enough; plays truant, loving the hard lessons of the street; school over, he has a half-hour of play, but must then travel his news route till six; after supper he has no taste for study; if he cannot go down into the street, he will go to bed. At fourteen, hating the school where he is beaten or scolded daily, he connives with his parents at certain falsehoods which secure his premature entrance into the factory. He works hard, and for a time happily enough; there is more freedom here than in the school. He discovers sex, passes through the usual chapter of accidents, and finally achieves manhood in the form of a sexual disease. He falls in love several times, and out as many times but one; he marries, shares his disease with his wife, and begets ten children - nearly all of them feeble, and two of them blind; he does not want so many children, but the priest has told him that religion commands it. He works harder to support them, but his health is giving way, and life becomes a heavy burden to him. The factory installs scientific management, and he finds himself performing the same operation every ten seconds from seven to twelve and from one to six - some three thousand times a day; he protests, but is told that science commands it. He joins a union, and goes out on strike; his family suffers severely, one of the children dying of malnutrition; he wins a wage-increase of five percent; his landlord raises his rent, and a month later his wife informs him that the prices of food and clothing have gone up six percent. His country goes to war about a piece of territory he has never heard of; his one fairly strong boy rushes off to the defense of the colors, returns (age twenty) with one leg and almost an arm, and sits in the house smoking, drinking, and dribbling in repetitious semi-torpor his memories of battle. Then comes street-corner talk of socialism, capitalism, and other things new and therefore hard to understand; a glimmer of hope, a cloud of doubt, then resignation. Four of the children die before they are twenty; two others become consumptive weaklings. The father is sent away from the factory because he is too old and feeble; he finds work in a saloon; drink helps him to slip down; he steals a bracelet from the factory-owner's kept woman, is arrested, tries to hang himself, but is discovered when half dead, and is restored to life against his will. He serves his sentence, returns to his family, and becomes a beggar. He dies of exposure and disease, and his widow is supported by two of his daughters, who have become successful prostitutes.

It is the picture of one life. And as you look at it you see beyond it the hundred thousand lives of which it is one; you see this suffering and meaninglessness as but one hundredth part of a thousandth part of the meaningless suffering of men; you hear the angry cries of the rebellious young, the drunken laughter of the older ones who have no more rebellion in them, the quiet weeping of the mothers of many children. Around you here you see the happy faces of young students, eloquent of comfortable homes; at your elbow a gentleman of family is writing a book on the optimism of Robert Browning. And then suddenly, beneath this world of leisure and learning, you feel the supporting brawn of the wearied workers; you vision the very pillars of this vast edifice held up painfully, hour after hour, on the backs of a million sweating men; your leisure is their labor, your learning is paid for by their ignorance, your luxury is their toil.

For a moment the great building seems to tremble, as if rebellion stirred beneath and upheaval was upon the world. Then it is still once more, and you and I are here with our thirty books.

One feels guilty of sentiment here (after reading Nietzsche!), and hurries back to the sober features of those crowded volumes. Here, in cold scientific statement, is our social problem: here are volumes biological on heredity, eugenics, dietetics, and disease; volumes sociological on marriage, prostitution, the family, the position of woman, contraception and the control of population; volumes psychological on education, criminology, and the replacement of supernatural by social religion; volumes economic on private property, poverty, child labor, industrial methods, arbitration, minimum wage, trusts, free trade, immigration, prohibition, war; volumes political on individualism and communism, anarchism and socialism, single tax, Darwinism and politics, democracy and aristocracy, patriotism, imperialism, electoral and administrative methods; methodological volumes on trade unions and craft unions, "direct action" and "political action," violence and non-resistance, revolution and reform. It is a discouraging maze; we plunge into it almost hopelessly. Several of these authors have schemes for taking the social machine apart, and a few even have schemes for putting it together again; hardly one of them remembers the old warning that this machine must be kept going while it is being repaired, And each of these solutions, as its author never suspects, is but an added problem.

Let us listen to these men for a while, let us follow them for a space, and see where they bring us out. They may not bring us out at all; but perhaps that is just what we need to see.

SOLUTIONS

Feminism

And first, with due propriety, let us listen to the case of woman versus the *status quo*. We imagine the argument as put by a studious and apparently harmless young lady. She begins gently and proceeds *crescendo*.

"The case for woman is quite simple; as simple as the case for democracy. We are human beings, we are governed, we are taxed; and we believe that just government implies the consent of the governed.

"We might have been content with the old life, had you masters of the world been content to leave us the old life. But you would not. Your system of industry has made the position of most young men so hopeless and insecure that they are year by year putting back the age of marriage. You have forced us out of our homes into your factories; and you have used us as a means of making still harder the competition for employment among the men. Your advocates speak of the sacredness of the home; and meanwhile you have dragged 5,000,000 English women out of their homes to be the slaves of your deadening machines.[307] You exalt marriage; and in this country one woman out of every ten is unmarried, and one out of every twenty married women works in your unclean shops. The vile cities born of your factory system have made life so hard for us, temptations so frequent, vice so attractive and convenient, that we cannot grow up among you without suffering some indelible taint.

---

307. Mrs. Gallichan, *The Truth about Woman*, New York. 1914, p. 281.

"Some of us go into your factories because we dread marriage, and some of us marry because we dread your factories. But there is not much to choose between them. If we marry we become machines for supplying another generation of workers and soldiers; and if we talk of birth control you arrest us. As if we had no right to all that science has discovered! And the horror of it is that while you forbid us to learn how to protect ourselves and our children from the evils of large families, you yourselves buy this knowledge from your physicians and use it; and one of your societies for the prevention of birth control has been shown to consist of members with an average of 1.5 children per family.[308] Your physicians meet in learned assemblies and vote in favor of maintaining the law which forbids the spread of this information; and then we find that physicians have the smallest average family in the community.[309] One must be a liar and a thief to fit comfortably into this civilization which you ask us to defend.

"But we are resolved to get this information; and all your laws to prevent us will only lessen our respect for law. We will not any longer bring children into the world unless we have some reasonable hope of giving them a decent life. And not only that: we shall end, too, the hypocrisies of marriage. If you will have monogamy you may have it; but if you continue merely to pretend monogamy we shall find a way of regaining our independence. We shall not rest until we have freed ourselves from the sting of your generosity; until our bread comes not from your hand in kindness but from the state or our employers in recognition of our work. Then we shall be free to leave you, and you free to leave us, as we were free to take one another at the beginning - so far, alas, as the categorical imperative of love left us free. And our children will not suffer; better for them that they see us part than that they live with us in the midst of hypocrisy and secret war.

"Because we want this freedom - to stay or to go - this freedom to know and control the vital factors of our lives, therefore we demand equal suffrage. It is but a little thing, a mere beginning; and beware how you betray your secrets in your efforts to bar us from this beginning. Are you afraid to share with us the power of the ballot? Do you confess so openly that you wish to command us without our consent, that you wish to use us for your secret ends? You dare not fight fair and in the open? Is the ballot a weapon which you use on us and will not let us use on you? It is so you conceive citizenship! Or will you ask us to believe that you are thinking not of your own interests but of posterity?

"But we shall get this from you, just as we get other things from you - by repetition. And then we shall go on to make the world more fit for women to live in: we shall force open all the avenues of life that have

---

308. Joe McCabe, *Tyranny of Shame*, London, 1916, p.171
309. Dr. Drysdale. *The Small Family System*, London, 1915.

been closed to us before, making us narrow and petty and dull. We shall compel your universities to admit us to their classes; we shall enter your professions, we shall compete with you for office, we shall win the experiences and dare the adventures which we need to make us your rivals in literature and philosophy and art. You say we cannot be your comrades, your friends; that we can be only tyrants or slaves; but what else can we be, with all the instructive wealth of life kept from us? You hide from us the great books that are being written today, and then you are surprised at our gossip, our silly scandal-mongering, our inability to converse with you on business and politics, on science and religion and philosophy; you will not let us grow, and then you complain because we are so small.

"But we want to grow now, we want to grow! We cannot longer be mothers only. The world does not need so many children; and even to bring up better children we must have a wider and healthier life. We must have our intellects stimulated more and our feelings less. We have burst the bonds of our old narrow world; we must explore everything now. It is too late to stop us; and if you try you will only make life a mess of hatred and conflict for us both. And after all, do you know why we want to grow? It is because we long for the day when we shall be no longer merely your mistresses, but also your friends."

Socialism

Another complainant: a young Socialist, such a man as works far into almost every night in the dingy office of his party branch, and devotes his Sundays to *Das Kapital;* bright-eyed, untouched by disillusionment; fired by the vision of a land of happy comrades.

"I agree with the young lady," he says, "the source of all our ills is the capitalist system. It was born of steam-driven machinery and conceived in *laissez-faire*. It saw the light in Adam Smith's England, ruined the health of the men of that country, and then came to America, where it grew fat' on 'liberty' and 'the right to do as one pleases with one's own.' It believed in competition - that is to say war - as its God, in whom all things lived and moved and sweated dividends; it made the acquisition of money, by no matter what means, the test of virtue and success, so that honest men became ashamed of themselves if they did not fail; it made all life a matter of 'push' and 'pull,' like the two sides of a door in one of those business palaces which make its cities great mazes of brick and stone rising like new Babels in the face of heaven. Its motto was, Beware of small profits; its aim was the greatest possible happiness of the smallest possible number. Out of' competition it begot the trust, the rebate, and the 'gentleman's agreement'; out of 'freedom of contract' it begot wage-s1avery; out of 'liberty, equality and fraternity' it begot an industrial feudalism worse than the old feudalism, based on the inheritance not of land, but of the living bodies and souls of thousands of men, women and children. When it came (in 1770) the annual income of England was $600,000,000; in 1901 the annual income of England was $8,000,000,000; the system has made a thousand millionaires, but it has left the people starving as before.[310] It has increased wages, and has increased prices a trifle more. It has improved the condition of the upper tenth of the workers, and has thrown the great remaining mass of the workers into a hell of torpor and despair. It has crowned all by inventing the myopic science of scientific management, whereby men are made to work at such speed, and with such rigid uniformity, that the mind is crazed, and the body is worn out twenty years before its time. It has made the world reek with poverty, and ugliness, and meanness, and the vulgarity of conspicuous wealth. It has made life intolerable and disgraceful to all but sheep and pigs.

"There is only one way of saving our civilization - such as there is of it - from wasting away through the parasitic degeneration of a few of its parts and the malnutrition of the rest; and that is by frankly abandoning this laissez-faire madness, and changing the state into a mechanism for the management of the nation's business. We workers must get hold of the offices, and turn government into administration. Without that our strikes and boycotts, our 'direct action' and economic organization, arrive at little result; every strike we 'win' means that prices will go up, and our time and energy - and dues - have gone to nothing but self-discipline in solidarity. We can control prices only by controlling monopolies; and we can control monopolies only by controlling government. That means politics, and it's a scheme that won't work until the proletariat get brains enough to elect honest and sensible men to office; but if they haven't the brains to do that they won't have the brains to do anything effective on the economic or any other field. We know how hard it is to get people to think; but we flatter ourselves that our propaganda is an educative force that grows stronger every year, and has already achieved such power as to decide the most important election held in this country since the Civil War.

"Already a large number of people have been educated - chiefly by our propaganda - to understand, for example, the economic greed that lies behind all wars. They perceive that so long as capital finds its highest rate of profit in the home market, capitalists see to it that peace remains secure; but that when capital has expanded to the point at which the rate of interest begins to fall, or when labor has ceased to be docile, because it has ceased to be unorganized and uninformed, capitalists then seek foreign markets and foreign investments, and soon require the help of war - that is, the lives of the workers at home - to help them enforce

310. Winston Churchill in Parliament, quoted by Schoonmaker, *The World-War and Beyond*, New York, 19115, p. 915.

their terms on foreign governments and peoples. Only the national ownership of capital can change that. We thought once that we were too civilized ever to go to war again; we begin to see that our industrial feudalism leads inevitably to war and armaments, and the intellectual stagna-
tion that comes from a militaristic mode of national life. We begin to see
all history as a Dark Age (with fitful intervals of light) - a long series of
wars in which men have killed and died for delusions, fighting to protect
the property of their exploiters. And it becomes a little clearer to us than
before that this awful succession of killings and robberies is no civilization
at all, and that we shall never have a civilization worthy of the name until
we transform our industrial war into the cooperative commonwealth, and
all 'foreigners' into friends."

Eugenics

"My dear young man," says the Eugenist at this point, "you must
study biology. Your plan for the improvement of mankind is all shot
through with childish ignorance of nature's way of doing things. Come into
my laboratory for a few years; and you will learn how little you can do by
merely changing the environment. It's nature that counts, not nurture.
Improvement depends on the elimination of the inferior, not on their reformation by Socialist leaflets or settlement work. What you have to do is
to find some substitute for that natural selection - the automatic and ruthless killing off of the unfit - which we are more and more frustrating with
our short-sighted charity. Humanitarianism must get informed. Our
squeamishness about interfering with the holy 'liberty of the individual' will
have to be moderated by some sense of the right of society to protect
itself from interference by the individual. Here are the feeble-minded, for
example; they breed more rapidly than healthy people do, and they
almost always transmit their defect. If you don't interfere with these people, if you don't teach them or force them to be childless, you will have an
increase in insanity along with the development of humanity. Think of
making a woman suffer to deliver into the world a cripple or an idiot. And
further, consider that the lowest eighth of the people produce one-half of
the next generation. The better people, the more vigorous and healthy
people, are refusing to have children; every year the situation is becoming more critical. City-life and factory-life make things still worse; young
men coming from the country plunge into the maelstrom of the city, then
into its femalestrom; they emerge with broken health, marry deformities
dressed up in the latest fashion, and produce children inferior in vigor and
ability to themselves. Given a hundred years more of this, and Western
Europe and America will be in a condition to be overcome easily by the
fertile and vigorous races of the East. That is what you have to think of.

The problem is larger than that of making poor people less poor; it is the problem of preserving our civilization. Your socialism will help, but it will be the merest beginning; it will be but an introduction to the socialization of selection, which is eugenics. We will prevent procreation by people who have a transmissible defect or disease; we will require certificates of health and clean ancestry before permitting marriage; we will encourage the mating, with or without love, of men and women possessed of energy and good physique. We will teach people, in Mr. Marett's phrase, to marry less with their eyes and more with their heads. It will take us a long while to put all this into effect; but we will put it. Time is on our side; every year will make our case stronger. Within half a century the educated world will come and beg us to guide them in a eugenic revolution."

Anarchism

A gentle anarchist:

"You do well to talk of revolution; but you do wrong to forget the individual in the race. Your eugenic revolution will not stop the exploitation of the workers by the manufacturers through the state. Give men justice and they will soon be healthy; give them the decent life which is the only just reward for their work, and you will not need eugenics. Instead of bothering about parasitic germs you should attend to parasitic exploiters; it is in this social parasitism that the real danger of degeneration lies. Continued injustice of employers to employees is splitting every western nation into factions; class-loyalty will soon be stronger than loyalty to the community; and the time will come when nations in which this civil war has not been superseded by voluntary mutual aid will crumble into oblivion.

"And yet men are willing to be loyal to the community, if the community is organized to give them justice. If exploitation were to cease there would be such bonds of brotherhood among men as would make the community practically everlasting. All you need do is to let men cooperate in freedom. They long to cooperate; all evolution shows a growth in the ability to cooperate; man surpassed the brute just because of this. Nor is law or state needed; coercive government is necessary only in societies founded on injustice. The state has always been an instrument of exploitation; and law is merely the organized violence of the ruling class. It is a subtle scheme; it enables industrial lords to do without any pangs of conscience what but for their statute-books might give them a qualm or two. Notice, for example, how perfectly Christian such slaughters as those in Colorado or Virginia can be made to appear - even to the slaughterers - by the delightful expedient of the statute-book. They kill and call it law, so that they may sleep.

"And then we are told that one must never use violence in labor disputes. But obviously it is precisely violence that is used against labor, and against the free spirit. As a matter of history, rebels did not begin to use violence on the authorities until the authorities had used violence on them. We feel ourselves quite justified in using any means of attack on a system so founded in coercion. The whole question with us is one not of morals but of expediency. We have been moral a little too long."

Individualism

"Precisely," says the Stirnerite anarchist;[311] "it is all a question of might, not of right; and we exploited ones may be as right as rectitude and never get anywhere unless we can rhyme a little might to our right. Each of us has a right to do whatever he is strong enough to do. "One gets farther with a handful of might than with a bagful of right." He who wants much, and knows how to get it, has in all times taken it, as Napoleon did the continent, and the French Algeria. Therefore the only point is that the respectful "lower classes" should at length learn to take for themselves what they want."

Individualism Again

And lastly, *Advocatus Diaboli*, Mr. *Status Quo:*
"I agree with you right heartily, Sir Stirnerite anarchist; it is time you children came to understand that everything is a question of power. Let the fittest survive and let us all use whatever means we find expedient. I am frank with you now; but you must not be surprised if tomorrow I write out a few checks for the salaries of the liars whom I have in my employ. Why should we tell the truth and go under? Surely you will understand that not all knowledge is good for all men. If it gives you satisfaction, for example, to spread information about birth control, you will not feel hurt if it gives us satisfaction to oppose you, for the sake of the future armies of unemployed without which our great scheme of industry would be seriously hampered.
"And I agree with your fellow anarchist, that the state is often a nuisance. I can make use of a little government; but when the state begins to tell me how to run my business, then I feel as if your criticism of the state is very just - and convenient. I am an individualist, a good old American individualist, like Jefferson and Emerson. The state can't manage industry half as well as we can. You know as our Socialists do not - that government ownership is only ownership by politicians, by Hinky-Dinks and Bath-house Johns; and I can tell you from intimate knowledge

---

311. "Stirnerite Anarchist" refers to Max Stirner, a German philosopher who argued that the state was an illegitimate institution; this element of his philosophy was adopted by anarchists (although Stirner himself was no anarchist and did, at times, criticize them).

of these people that they will do anything for money except efficient administrative work.

"Your scheme of having the workers take over the industries is a good scheme - for the millennium. Where would you get men to direct you? They come to us because we pay them well; if your syndicalist shops would pay them as well as we do, they would be the beginning of a new aristocracy; if you think these clever men will work for 'honor' you are leaning on an airy dream. Destroy private property and you will have a nation of hoboes and Hindus.

"As to exploitation, what would you have? We are strong, and you are weak; it is the law of nature that we should use you, just as it is the law of nature that one species should use the weaker species as its prey. The weaker will always suffer, with or without law. Even if all bellies are full, the majority will envy the intellectual power of their betters, and will suffer just as keenly on the intellectual plane as they do now on the physical. The alternative of the underdog is to get intelligence and power, or 'stay put.'

"My advice, then, is to let things be. You can change the superficial conditions of the struggle for existence and for power, but the fundamental facts of it will remain. Monarchy, aristocracy, democracy - it's all the same. The most powerful will rule, whether by armies or by newspapers; it makes no difference if God is on the side of the biggest battalions, or the side of the biggest type. We bought the battalions; we buy the type.

"Come, let us get back to our business."

Dissolutions

Here is a *reductio ad absurdum* of our social *'isms;* and here is the history of many a social rebel. From dissatisfaction to socialism, from socialism to anarchism, from anarchism to Stirnerism, from Stirnerism and the cult of the ego to Nietzsche and the right to exploit - so has many a man made the merry-go-round of thought and come back wearily at last to the *terra firma* of the thing that is. We sail into the sea of social controversy without chart or compass or rudder; and though we encounter much wind, we never make the port of our desire. We need maps, and instruments, and knowledge; we need to make inquiries, to face our doubts, to define our purposes; we shall have to examine more ruthlessly our preconceptions and hidden premises, to force into the light the wishes that secretly father our illegitimate thoughts. We must ask ourselves questions that will reach down to the tenderest roots of our philosophies.

You are a feminist, let us say. Very well. Have you ever considered the sociological consequences of that very real disintegration of the

"home" which an advancing feminism implies? Granted that this disintegration has been begun by the industrial revolution. Do you want it to go
on more rapidly? Do you want women to become more like men? Do you
think that the "new woman" will care to have children? It is surely better
for the present comfort of our society that there should be a considerable
fall in the birth rate; but will that expose the people of Europe and America
to absorption by the races of the East? You argue that the case for feminism is as simple as the case for democracy; but is the case for democracy simple? Is democracy competent? Is it bringing us where we want to
go? Or is it a sort of collective determination to drift with the tide - a sort
of magnified *laissez-faire*? And as to "rights" and "justice," how do you
answer Nietzsche's contention that the more highly organized species,
sex, or class, must by its very nature use, command, and exploit the less
highly organized species, sex, or class?

You are a Socialist; and you yearn for a Utopia of friends and equals;
but will you, to make men equal, be compelled to chain the strength of the
strong with many laws and omnipresent force? Will you sacrifice the
superiority of the chosen few to the mediocrity of the many? Will you, to
control the exploiter, be obliged to control all men, even in detail? Will
your socialism really bring the slavery and servile state that Spencer and
Chesterton and Belloc fear? Is further centralization of government desirable? Have you considered sufficiently the old difficulty about the stimulus to endeavor in a society that should restrict private property to a minimum and prohibit inheritance? Have you arranged to protect your cooperative commonwealth by limiting immigration - from Europe and from
heaven?[312] Are you not, in general, exaggerating the force of the
aggregative as against the segregative tendencies in human nature? And
do you think that a change of laws can make the weak elude the exploit-
ing arm of the strong? Will not the strongest men always make whatever
laws are made, and rule wherever men are ruled? Can any government
stand that is not the expression of the strongest forces in the community? And if the strongest force be organized labor, are you sure that organized labor will not exploit and tyrannize? Will the better organized and
skilled workers be "just" to the unskilled and imperfectly organized workers? And what do you mean by "justice"?

And as to the eugenist, surely it is unnecessary to expose his unpre-
paredness to meet the questions which his program raises. Questions, for
example, as to what "units" of character to breed for, if there are such
"units"; whether definite breeding for certain results would forfeit adaptive
plasticity; whether compulsory sterilization is warranted by our knowledge
of heredity; whether serious disease is not often associated with genius;
whether the native mental endowments of rich and poor are appreciably

---

312. Carver, *Essays in Social Justice*, New York, 1915, p. 261.

different, and whether the "comparative infertility of the upper classes" is really making for the deterioration of the race; whether progress depends on racial changes so much as on changes in social institutions and traditions. And so on.

And the anarchist, whom one loves if only for the fervor of his hope and the beauty of his dream, - the anarchist falters miserably in the face of interrogation. If all laws were to be suspended tomorrow, all coercion of citizen by state, how long would it be before new laws would arise? Would the aforementioned strong cease to be strong and the weak cease to be weak? Would people be willing to forego private property? Are not belief and disbelief in private property determined less by logic and "justice" than by one's own success or failure in the acquisition of private property? Do only the weak and uncontrolled advocate absolute lack of restraint? Do most men want liberty so much that they will tolerate chaos and a devil-take-the-hindmost individualism for the sake of it? Can it be, after all, that freedom is a negative thing, that what men want is, for some, achievement, for others, peace - and that for these they will give even freedom? What if a great number of people dread liberty, and are not at all so sensitive to restraint and commandment as the anarchist? Perhaps only children and geniuses can be truly anarchistic? Perhaps freedom itself is a problem and not a solution? Does the mechanization, through law and custom, of certain elements in our social behavior, like the mechanization, through habit and instinct, of certain elements in individual behavior, result in greater freedom for the higher powers and functions? Again, to have freedom for all, all must be equal; but does not development make for differentiation and inequality? Consider the America of three hundred years ago; a nation of adventurous settlers, hardly any of them better off than any other - all of a class, all on a level; and see what inequalities and castes a few generations have produced! Is there a necessary antithesis between liberty and order, freedom and control, or are order and control the first condition of freedom? Does not law serve many splendid purposes - could it not serve more? Is the state necessary so long as there are long-eared and long-fingered gentry?

As for your revolutions, who profits by them? The people who have suffered, or the people who have thought? Is a revolution, so far as the poor are concerned, merely the dethronement of one set of rulers or exploiters so that another set may have a turn? Do not most revolutions, like that which wished to storm heaven by a tower, end in a confusion of tongues? And after each outbreak do not the workers readapt themselves to their new slavery with that ease and torpid patience which are the despair of every leader, until they are awakened by another quarrel among their masters?

One could fling about such questions almost endlessly, till every *'ism* should disappear under interrogation points. Every such *'ism*, clearly, is but a half-truth, an arrested development, suffering from malinformation. One is reminded of the experiment in which a psychologist gave a ring-puzzle to a monkey, and - in another room - a like puzzle to a university professor: the monkey fell upon the puzzle at once with teeth and feet and every manner of hasty and haphazard reaction, until at last the puzzle, dropped upon the floor, came apart by chance; the professor sat silent and motionless before the puzzle, working out in thought the issue of many suggested solutions, and finally, after forty minutes, touched it to undo it at a stroke. Our *'isms* are simian reactions to the social puzzle. We jump at conclusions, we are impinged upon extremes, we bound from opposite to opposite, we move with blinders to a passion-colored goal. Some of us are idealists, and see only the beautiful desire; some of us are realists, and see only the dun and dreary fact; hardly any of us can look fact in the face and see through it to that which it might be. We "bandy half-truths" for a decade and then relapse into the peaceful insignificance of conformity.[313]

It dawns on students of social problems, as it dawned long since on philosophers, that the beginning of their wisdom is a confession of their ignorance. We know now that the thing we need, and for lack of which we blunder valiantly into futility, is not good intentions but informed intelligence. All problems are problems of education; all the more so in a democracy. Not because education can change the original nature of man, but because intelligent cooperation can control the stimuli which determine the injuriousness or beneficence of original dispositions. Impulse is not the enemy of intelligence; it is its raw material. We desire knowledge - and particularly knowledge of ourselves - so that we may know what external conditions evoke destructive, and what conditions evoke constructive, responses. We do not, for example, expect intelligence to eradicate pugnacity; we do not want it to do so; but we want to eradicate the environmental conditions which turn this impulse to wholesale suicide. Men should fight; it is the essence of their value that they are willing to fight; the problem of intelligence is to discuss and to create means for the diversion of pugnacity to socially helpful ends. Character is

313. The "experimental attitude . . . substitutes detailed analyses for wholesale1e assertions, specific inquiries for temperamental convictions, small facts for opinions whose size is in precise ratio to their vagueness. It is within the social sciences, in morals, politics, and education, that thinking still goes on by large antitheses, by theoretical oppositions of order and freedom, individualism and socialism, culture and utility, spontaneity and discipline, actuality and tradition. The field of the physical sciences was once occupied by similar 'total' views, whose emotional appeal was inversely as their intellectual clarity. But with the advance of the experimental method, the question has ceased to be which one of two rival claimants has a right to the field. It has become a question of clearing up a confused subject matter by attacking it bit by bit. I do not know a case where the final result was anything like victory for one or another among the pre-experimental notions. All of them disappeared because they became increasingly irrelevant to the situation discovered, and with their detected irrelevance they became unmeaning and uninteresting." - Professor John Dewey. *New Republic*. Feb. 3. 1917.

per se neither good nor bad, but becomes one or the other according to the nature of the stimuli presented. What we call moral reform, then, waits on information and consequent remolding of the factors determining the direction of our original dispositions. We become "better" men and women only so far as we become more intelligent. Just as psychoanalysis can, in some measure, reconstruct the personal life, so social analysis can reconstruct social life and turn into productive channels the innocent but too often destructive forces of original nature.[314]

Our problem, then, to repeat once more our central theme, is to facilitate the growth and spread of intelligence. With this definition of the issue we come closer to our thesis - that the social problem must be approached through philosophy, and philosophy through the social problem.

---

314. All this has been indicated - with, however, too little emphasis on the reconstructive function of intelligence - by Bertrand Russell in *Principles of Social Reconstruction* (London. 1916); and more popularly by Max Eastman in *Understanding Germany* (New York, 1916); it has been put very briefly again and again by Professor Dewey, - e.g., in an essay on "Progress" in the *International Journal of Ethics*, April, 1916.

CHAPTER SEVEN
THE RECONSTRUCTIVE FUNCTION OF
PHILOSOPHY

Epistemologs

Now there are a great many people who will feel no thrill at all at the mention of philosophy, who will rather consider themselves excused by the very occurrence of the word from continuing on the road which this discussion proposes to travel. No man dares to talk of philosophy in these busy days except after an apologetic preface; philosophers themselves have come to feel that their thinking is so remote from practical endeavor that they have for the most part abandoned the effort to relate their work to the concrete issues of life. In the eyes of the man who does things philosophy is but an aerial voyaging among the mists of transcendental dialectic, or an ineffective moralizing substitute for supernatural religion. Philosophy was once mistress of all the disciplines of thought and search; now none so poor to do her reverence.

There is no way of meeting this indictment other than to concede it. It is true. It is mild. Only a lover of philosophy can know - with the intimacy of a *particeps criminis* - how deeply philosophy has fallen from her ancient heights. Looking back to Greece we find that philosophy there was a real pursuit of wisdom, a very earnest effort to arrive by discussion and self-criticism at a way of life, a *philosophia vitae magistra*, a knowledge of the individual and social good and of the means thereto, a conscious direction of social institutions to ethical ends; philosophy and life in those days were bound up with one another as mechanics is now bound up with efficient construction. Even in the Middle Ages philosophy meant coordinate living, synthetic behavior; with all their reputation for cobweb spinning, the Scholastics were much closer to life in their thinking than most modern philosophers have been in theirs.

The lapse of philosophy from her former significance and vitality is the result of the exaggerated emphasis placed on the epistemological problem by modern thinkers; and this in turn is in great part due to the difficulties on which Descartes stumbled in his effort to reconcile his belief in mechanism with his desire to placate the Jesuits: How minor a role is played by the problems of the relation between subject and object, the validity of knowledge, epistemological realism and idealism, in a frankly mechanist philosophy, appears in Bacon, Hobbes, and Spinoza;[315] these men - deducting Bacon's astute obeisance to theology - know what they want and say what they mean; they presume, with a maturity so natural as to be mistaken for naïveté, that the validity of thought is a matter to be decided by action rather than by theory; they take it for granted that the supreme and ultimate purpose of philosophy is not analysis but synthesis, not the intellectual categorizing of experience but the intelligent reconstruction of life. Indeed, as one pursues this clew through the devious - almost stealthy - course of modern speculation it appears that no small part of the epistemological development has been made up of the oscillations, compromises, and obscurities natural in men who were the exponents and the victims of a painful transition. Civilization was passing from one intellectual basis to another; and in these weird epistemologs the vast process came uncomfortably to semi-consciousness. They were old bottles bursting with new wine; and their tragedy was that they knew it. They clung to the old world even while the new one was swimming perilously into their ken; they found a pitiful solace in the old phrases, the old paraphernalia of a dead philosophy; and in the suffering of their readjustment there was, quite inevitably, some measure of self-deception.

And that is why they are so hard to understand. Even so subtle a thinker as Santayana finds them too difficult, and abandons them in righteous indignation. There is no worse confounding of confusion than self-deception: let a man be honest with himself, and he may lie with tolerable intelligibility and success; but let him be his own dupe and he may write a thousand critiques and never get himself understood. Indeed, some of them do not want to be understood, they only want to be believed. Hegel, for example, was not at all surprised to find that no one understood him; he would have been surprised and chagrined to find that some one had. Obscurity can cover a multitude of sins.

Add to this self-befoggery the appalling *historismus* (as Eucken calls it), the strange lifeless interest in the past for its own sake, the petty poring over problems of text and minutia of theory in the classics of speculation - and the indictment of philosophy as a useless appanage of the idle rich gains further ground. We do not seem to understand how much of the past is dead, how much of it is but a drag on the imaginative courage that dares to think of a future different from the past, and better. Philosophy is too much a study of the details of superseded systems; it is too little the study of the miraculous living moment in which the past melts into the present and the future finds creation. Most people have an invincible habit of turning their backs to the future; they like the past because the future is an adventure. So with most philosophers today; they like to

---

315. This is not a defense of mechanism or materialism; it is a plea for a better perspective in philosophy.

write analyses of Kant, commentaries on Berkeley, discussions of Plato's myths; they are students remembering, they have not yet become men thinking. They do not know that the work of philosophy is in the street as well as in the library, they do not feel and understand that the final problem of philosophy is not the relation of subject and object but the misery of men.

And so it is well that philosophy, such as it chiefly is in these days, should be scorned as a busy idler in a world where so much work is asking to be done.

Philosophy was vital in Plato's day; so vital that some philosophers were exiled and others put to death. No one would think of putting a philosopher to death today. Not because men are more delicate about killing; but because there is no need to kill that which is already dead.[316]

Philosophy as Control

But after all, this is not a subject for rhetoric so much as for resolution. Here we are again in our splendid library; here we sit, financially secure, released from the material necessities of life, to stand apart and study, to report and help and state and solve; under us those millions holding us aloft so that we may see for them, dying by the thousand so that we may find the truth that will make the others free; and what do we do? We make phrases like "*esse est percipi*," "synthetic judgments *a priori*," and "being is nothing"; we fill the philosophic world with great Saharas of Kantiana; we write epistemology for two hundred years. Surely there is but one decent thing for us to do: either philosophy is of vital use to the community, or it is not. If it is not, we will abandon it; if it is, then we must seek that vital use and show it. We have been privileged to study and think and travel and learn the world; and now we stand gaping before it as if there were nothing wrong, as if nothing could be done, as if nothing should be done. We are expert eyes, asked to point the way; and all that we report is that there is nothing to see, and nowhere to go. We are without even a partial sense of the awful responsibility of intelligence.

It is time we put this problem of knowledge, even the problem of the validity of knowledge, into the hands of science. How we come to know, what the process of knowledge is, what "truth" is - all these are questions of fact; they are problems for the science of psychology, they are not problems for philosophy. This continual sharpening of the knife, as Lotze put it, becomes tiresome - almost pathetic - if, after all, there is no cutting

316. It would be invidious to name the exceptions which one is glad to remember here; but it is in place to say that the practical arrest of Bertrand Russell is a sign of resuscitation on the part of philosophy - a sign for which all lovers of philosophy should be grateful. When philosophers are once more feared, philosophy will once more be respected.

done. Like Faust, who found himself when, blinded by the sun, he turned his face to the earth, so we shall have to forget our epistemological heaven and remember mother earth; we shall have to give up our delightful German puzzles and play our living part in the flow of social purpose. Philosophers must once more learn to live.

To make such a demand for a new direction of philosophy to life is after all only a development of pragmatism, turning that doctrine of action as the test and significance of thought to uses not so individual as those in which William James found its readiest application. If philosophy has meaning, it must be as life become aware of its purposes and possibilities, it must be as life cross-examining life for the sake of life; it must be as specialized foresight for the direction of social movement, as reconstructive intelligence in conscious evolution. Man finds himself caught in a flux of change; he studies the laws operating in the flux; studying, he comes to understand; understanding, he comes to control; controlling, he comes face to face with the question of all questions, for what? Where does he wish to go, what does he want to be? It is then that man puts his whole experience before him in synthetic test; then that he gropes for meanings, searches for values, struggles to see and define his course and goal; then that he becomes philosopher. Consider these questions of goal and course as questions asked by a society, and the social function of philosophy appears. Science enlightens means, philosophy must enlighten ends. Science informs, philosophy must form. A philosopher is a man who remakes himself; the social function of philosophy is to remake society.

Have we yet felt the full zest of that brave discovery of the last century - that purpose is not in things but in us? What a declaration of independence there is in that simple phrase, what liberation of a fettered thought to dare all ventures of creative endeavor! Here at last is man's coming-of-age! Well, now that we have won this freedom, what shall we do with it? That is the question which freedom begets, often as its Frankenstein; for unless freedom makes for life, freedom dies. Once our sloth and cowardice might have pleaded the uselessness of effort in a world where omnipotent purpose lay outside of us, superimposed and unchangeable; now that we can believe that divinity is in ourselves, that purpose and guidance are through us, we can no longer shirk the question of reconstruction. The world is ours to do with what we can and will. Once we believed in the unchangeable environment - that new ogre that succeeded to the Absolute - and (as became an age of *laissez-faire*) we thought that wisdom lay in meeting all its demands; now we know that environments can be remade; and we face the question: how shall we remake ours?

This is preeminently a problem in philosophy; it is a question of values. If the world is to be remade, it will have to be under the guidance of philosophy.

Philosophy as a Mediator between Science and Statesmanship

But why philosophy? Why will not science do? Philosophy dreams, while one by one the sciences which she nursed steal away from her and go down into the world of fact and achievement. Why should not science be called upon to guide us into a better world?

Because science becomes more and more a fragmentated thing, with ever less coordination, ever less sense of the whole. Our industrial system has forced division of labor here, as in the manual trades, almost to the point of idiocy: let a man seek to know everything about something, and he will soon know nothing about anything else; efficiency will swallow up the man. Because of this shredded science we have great zoologists talking infantile patriotism about the war, and great electricians who fill sensational sheets with details of their trips to heaven. We live in a world where thought breaks into pieces, and coordination ebbs; we flounder into a chaos of hatred and destruction because synthetic thinking is not in fashion.

Consider, for example, the problem of monopoly: we ask science what we are to do here; why is it that after we have listened to the economist, and the historian, and the lawyer, and the psychologist, we are hardly better off than before? Because each of these men speaks in ignorance of what the others have discovered. We must find some way of making these men acquainted with one another before they can become really useful to large social purposes; we must knock their heads together. We want more uniters and coordinators, less analyzers and accumulators. Specialization is making the philosopher a social necessity of the very first importance.

This does not mean that we must put the state into the hands of the epistemologists. Hardly. The type of philosopher who must be produced will be a man too close to life to spend much time on merely analytical problems. He will feel the call of action, and will automatically reject all knowledge that does not point to deeds. The essential feature of him will be grasped; he will have his net fixed for the findings of those sciences which have to do, not with material reconstructions, but with the discovery of the secrets of human nature. He will know the essentials of biology and psychology, of sociology and history, of economics and politics; in him these long-divorced sciences will meet again and make one another fertile once more. He will busy himself with Mendel and Freud, Sumner and Veblen, and will scandalously neglect the Absolute. He will study the needs and exigencies of his time, he will consider the Utopias men make, he will see in them the suggestive pseudopodia of political theory, and will learn from them what men at last desire. He will sober the vision with fact, and find a focus for immediate striving. With this focus he will be able to coordinate his own thinking, to point the nose of science to a goal; science becoming thereby no longer inventive and instructive merely, but preventive and constructive. And so fortified and unified he will preach his gospel, talking not to students about God, but to statesmen about men.

For we come again - ever and ever again - to Plato: unless wisdom and practical ability, philosophy and statesmanship, can be more closely bound together than they are, there will be no lessening of human misery. Think of the learning of scientists and the ignorance of politicians! You see all these agitated, pompous men, making laws at the rate of some ten thousand a year; you see those quiet, unheard of, underpaid seekers in the laboratories of the world; unless you can bring these two groups together through coordination and direction, your society will stand still forever, however much it moves. Philosophy must take hold; it must become the social direction of science, it must become, strange to say, applied science.

We stand today in social science where Bacon stood in natural science: we seek a method first for the elucidation of causes, and second for the transformation, in the light of this knowledge, of man's environment and man. "We live in the stone age of political science," says Lester Ward; "in politics we are still savages."[317] Our political movements are conceived in impulse and developed in emotion; they end in fission and fragmentation because there is no thought behind them. Who will supply thinking to these instincts, direction to this energy, light to this wasted heat? Our young men talk only of ideals, our politicians only of fact; who will interpret to the one the language of the other? What is it, too, that statesmen need if not that saving sense of the whole which makes philosophy, and which philosophy makes? Just as philosophy without statesmanship is - let us say - epistemology, so statesmanship without philosophy is - American politics. The function of the philosopher, then, is to do the listening to today's science, and then to do the thinking for tomorrow's statesmanship. The philosophy of an age should be the organized foresight of that age, the interpreter of the future to the present. "Selection adapts man to yesterday's conditions, not to today's";[318] the organized foresight of conscious evolution will adapt man to the conditions of tomorrow. And an ounce of foresight is worth a ton of morals.

---

317. *American Journal of Sociology*. March. 1905, p. 645.
318. Ross, *Social Control*, New York, 1906. p. 9.

CHAPTER EIGHT
ORGANIZED INTELLIGENCE

The Need

Intelligence is organized experience; but intelligence itself must be organized. Consider the resources of the unused intelligence of the world; intelligence potential but undeveloped; intelligence developed but isolated; intelligence allowed to waste itself in purely personal pursuits, unasked to enter into cooperation for larger ends. Consider the Platos fretting in exile while petty politicians rule the world; consider Montaigne, and Hobbes, and Hume, and Carlyle, and the thousand other men whose genius was left to grow - or die - in solitude or starvation; consider the vast number of university-trained minds who are permitted, for lack of invitation and organized facilities, to slip into the world of profit and loss and destructively narrow intent; consider the expert ability in all lines which can be found in the faculties of the world, and which goes to training an infinitesimal fraction of the community. The thought of university graduates, of university faculties, of university-trained investigators, has had a rapidly growing influence in the last ten years in America; and because it is an influence due to enlightenment it is fundamentally an influence for "good." It was this influence that showed when President Wilson said that the eight-hour day was demanded by the informed opinion of the time. The sources of such influence have merely been touched; they are deep; we must find a way to make informed opinion more articulate and powerful. "The most valuable knowledge consists of methods," said Nietzsche;[319] and the most valuable methods are methods of organization, whether of data or of men. Organization's the thing. Economic forces are organized; the forces of intelligence are not. To organize intelligence; that is surely one method of approach to the social problem; and what if, indeed, it be the very heart and substance of the social problem?

Now a very easy way of making the propounder of such an organization feel unusually modest is to ask him that little trouble-making question, *How?* To answer that would be to answer almost everything that can be answered. Here are *opera basilica* again, for what are we doing, after all, but trying to take Francis Bacon seriously? Of course the difficulty in organizing intelligence is how to know who are intelligent, and how to get enough people to agree with you that you know. If each man's self-valu-

---

319. *Will to Power*, § 469.

ation were accepted, our organization would be rather bulky. Are there any men very widely recognized as intelligent, who could be used as the nucleus of an organization? There are individual men so recognized - Edison, for example, and, strange to say, one or two men who by accident are holding political office. But these are stray individuals; are there any groups whose average of intelligence is highly rated by a large portion of the community? There are. Physicians are so rated; so much so that by popular usage they have won almost a monopoly on the once more widely used term doctor. University professors are highly rated. Let us take the physicians and the professors; here is a nucleus of recognized intelligence.

There are objections, here, of course; some one urges that many physicians are quacks, another that professors are rated as intelligent, but only in an impractical sort of way. Perhaps we shall find some scheme for eliminating the quacks; but the professors present a difficult problem. It is true that they suffer from intellectualism, academitis, overfondness for theories, and other occupational diseases; it is true that the same people who stand in awe of the very word *professor* would picture the article indicated by the word as a thin, round-shouldered, be-spectacled ninny, incapable of finding his way alone through city streets, and so immersed in the stars that he is sooner or later submerged in a well. But what if this quality of detachment, of professorial calm, be just one of the qualities needed for the illumination of our social problem? Perhaps we have too much emotion in these questions, and need the colder light of the man who is trained to use his "head" and not his "heart." Perhaps the most useful thing in the world for our purpose is this terribly dispassionate, coldly scrutinizing professor. We need men as impartial and clear-eyed as men come; and whatever a professor may *say*, yet he *sees* his field more clearly and impartially than any other group of men whatever. Let the professors stay.

And so we have our physicians and our professors - say all physicians and professors who have taught or practiced three years in institutions, or as the graduates of institutions, of recognized standing. And now let us dream our dream.

The Organization of Intelligence

These men, through meetings and correspondence, organize themselves into a "Society for Social Research"; they begin at once to look for an "inspired millionaire" to finance the movement for six months or so; they advertise themselves diligently in the press, and make known their intention to get together the best brains of the country to study the facts and possibilities of the social problem. And then - a difficult point - they

face the task of arranging some more or less impersonal method of decid-
ing who are the intelligent people and who not. They ask themselves just
what kind of information a man should be expected to have, to fit him for
competent handling of social questions; and after long discussions they
conclude that such a man should be well trained in one - and acquainted
with the general findings of the others - of what we may call the social disciplines: biology, psychology, sociology, history, economics, law, politics,
philosophy, and perhaps more. They formulate a long and varied test for
the discovery of fitness in these fields; and they arrange that every university in the country shall after plentiful advertisement and invitation to
all and sundry, give these tests, and pay the expenses incurred by any
needy candidate who shall emerge successful from the trial. In this way
men whose studies have been private, and unadorned with academic
degree, are to find entrance to the Society.

It is recognized that the danger of such a test lies in the premium
which it sets on the bookish as against the practical man: on the man
whose knowledge has come to him in the classroom or the study, as
against the man who has won his knowledge just by living face to face
with life. There are philosophers who have never heard of Kant, and psychologists who have been Freudians for decades without having ever
read a book. A society recruited by such a test will be devoid of artists and
poets, may finally eliminate all but fact-gathering dry-as-dusts, and so end
deservedly in nothing. And yet some test there must be, to indicate, however crudely, one's fitness or unfitness to take part in this work; the alternative would be the personal choice of the initial few, whose prejudices
and limitations would so become the constitution and by-laws of the society. Perhaps, too, some way may appear of using the artists and poets,
and the genius who knows no books.

Well, the tests are given; the original nucleus of physicians and professors submit themselves to these tests, and some, failing, are eliminated; other men come, from all fields of work, and from them a number survive the ordeal and pass into the Society. So arises a body of say 5,000
men, divided into local groups but working in unison so far as geographical separateness will permit; and to them now come, impressed with their
earnestness, a wealthy man, who agrees to finance the Society for such
time as may be needed to test its usefulness.

Now what does our Society do?

It seeks information. That, and not a program, is the fruitful beginning
of reform. "Men are willing to investigate only the small things of life," says
Samuel Butler; this Society for Social Research is prepared and resolved
to investigate anything that has vital bearing on the social problem; it
stands ready to make enemies, ready to soil its hands. It appoints committees to gather and formulate all that biologists can tell of human origin

and the innate impulses of men; all that psychology in its varied branches can tell of human behavior; all that sociology knows of how and why human societies and institutions rise and fall; all that medicine can tell of social ills and health; it appoints committees to go through all science with the loadstone of the social purpose, picking up this fact here and that one there; committees to study actual and proposed forms of government, administrative and electoral methods; committees to investigate marriage, eugenics, prostitution, poverty, and the thousand other aspects and items of the social problem; committees to call for and listen to responsible expressions of every kind of opinion; committees to examine and analyze social experiments, profit-sharing plans, Oneida communities; even a committee on Utopia, before which persons with schemes and *'isms* and perfect cities in their heads may freely preach their gospel. In short this Society becomes the organized eye and ear of the community, ready and eager to seek out all the facts of human life and business that may enlighten human will.

And having found the facts it publishes them. Its operations show real earnestness, sincerity, and ability; and in consequence it wins such prestige that its reports find much heralding, synopsis, and comment in the press. But in addition to that it buys, for the first day of every month, a half-page of space in several of the more widely circulated periodicals and journals of the country, and publishes its findings succinctly and intelligibly. It gives full references for all its statements of fact; it makes verification possible for all doubters and deniers. It includes in each month's report a reliable statement of the year's advances in some one of the social disciplines, so that its twelve reports in any year constitute a record of the socially vital scientific findings of the year. It limits itself strictly to verifiable information, and challenges demonstration of humanly avoidable partiality. And it takes great care that its reports are couched not in learned and technical language but in such phraseology as will be intelligible to the graduates of an average grammar school. That is central.[320]

Information of Panacea

Without some such means of getting and spreading information there is no hope for fundamental social advance. We have agreed, have we not, that to make men happier and more capable we must divert their socially injurious impulses into beneficent channels; that we can do this only by studying those impulses and controlling the stimuli which arouse them; that we can control those stimuli only by studying the varied factors

---

320. An organization very similar to what Durant envisioned has existed since 1961. *The World Policy Institute*, based in New York, is a think tank and policy center uniting experts in the fields of economics, philosophy, journalism, and politics; the group releases reports and opinions on global issues concerning migration, climate change, technology, economic development, human rights, and counter-terrorism.

of the environment and the means of changing them; in short, that at the bottom of the direction of impulse lies the necessity, of knowledge, of information spread to all who care to receive it. Autocracy may improve the world without spreading enlightenment; but democracy cannot. *Delenda est ignorantia*.[321]

This, after all, is a plan for the democratization of aristocracy; it is Plato translated into America. It utilizes superior intelligence and gives it voice, but sanctions no change that has not received the free consent of the community, It gives the aristocracy of intellect the influence and initiative which crude democracy frustrates; but it avoids the corruption that usually goes with power, by making this influence work through the channels of persuasion rather than compulsion. It counteracts the power of wealth to disseminate partisan views through news items and editorials, and relies on fact to get the better at last of double-leaded prejudice. It rests on the faith that lies will out.

Would the mass of the people listen to such reports? Consider, first, the repute that attaches to the professorial title. Let a man write even the sorriest nonsense but sign himself as one of the faculty of some responsible institution, and he will find a hearing; the reader, perhaps, need not go far to find an example. In recent industrial and political issues, the pronouncements of a few professors carried very great weight; and there are some modest purveyors of so supposedly harmless a thing as philosophy whose voice is feared by all interests that prosper in the dark. Will the combined reputation of the most enlightened men in the country mean less? A report published by this Society for Social Research will mean that a large body of intelligent men have from their number appointed three or five or ten to find the facts of a certain situation or dispute; these appointed men will, if they report hastily, or carelessly, or dishonestly, impair the repute of all their fellows in the Society; they will take care, then, and will probably find honesty as good a policy as some of us pretend it to be. With every additional report so guarded from defect the repute of the society will grow until it becomes the most powerful intellectual force in the world.

When one reflects how many pages of misrepresentation were printed in the papers of only one city in the presidential campaign of 1916, and then imagines what would have been the effect of a mere statement of facts on both sides - the records of the candidates and the parties, their acknowledged connections, friends and enemies, their expressed principles and programs, the facts about the tariff, the German issue, international law, the railway-brotherhood dispute, and so forth - one begins to appreciate the importance of information. After the initial and irrevocable differences of original nature, nothing is so vital as the spread of enlight-

---

321. Barker, *Political Thought of Plato and Aristotle*, p. 80

enment; and nothing offers itself so well to organized effort. Eugenics is weak because it has no thought-out program; 'isms rise and fall because people are not informed. Let who can, improve the native qualities of men; but that aside, the most promising plan is the dissemination of fact.

Such a society for research would be a sort of social consciousness, a "mind of the race." It would make social planning possible for the first time; it would make history conscious. It would look ahead and warn; it would point the nose of the community to unwelcome but important facts; it would examine into such statements as that of Sir William Ramsay, that England's coal fields will be exhausted in one hundred and seventy-five years; and its warnings, backed by the prestige of its expert information, would perhaps avert the ravages of social waste and private greed. Nature, said Lester Ward, is a spendthrift, man an economizer. But economy means prevision, and social economy means organized provision. Here would be not agitation, not propaganda, not moralizing, but only clarification; these men would be "merchants of light," simply giving information so that what men should do they might do knowingly and not in the dark.

Indeed, if one can clarify one need not agitate. Just to state facts is the most terrible thing that can be done to an injustice. Sermons and stump-speeches stampede the judgment for a moment, but the sound of their perorations still lingers in the air when reaction comes. Fact has this advantage over rhetoric, that time strengthens the one and weakens the other. Tell the truth and time will be your eloquence.

Let us suppose that our Society has existed some three years; let us suppose that on the first day of every month it has spread through the press simple reports of its investigations, simple accounts of socially significant work in science, and simple statements of fact about the economic and political issues of the day; let us suppose that by far the greater part of these reports have been conscientious and accurate and clear. Very well: in the course of these three years a large number of mentally alert people all over the country will have developed the habit of reading these monthly reports; they will look forward to them, they will attach significance to them, they will herald them as events, almost as decisions. In any question of national policy its statements will influence thousands and thousands of the more independent minds. Let us calculate the number of people who, in these United States, would be reached by such reports; let us say the reports are printed in three or four New York dailies, having a total circulation of one million; in other dailies throughout the country totaling some five million circulation; and in one or more weeklies or monthlies with a large or a select circulation. One may perhaps say that out of the seven or eight million people so reached (mostly adult males), five percent will be so influenced by the increasing prestige of the Society that they will read the reports. Of these four hundred thousand readers it is reasonable to suppose that three hundred thousand will be voters, and not only voters but men of influence among their fellows. These men will each of them be a medium through which the facts reported will be spread; it is not too much to say that the number of American voters influenced directly or indirectly by these reports will reach to a million.[322] Now imagine the influence of this million of voters on a presidential election. Their very existence would be a challenge; candidates would have them in mind when making promises and criticisms; parties would think of them when formulating policies and drawing up platforms; editors would beware of falling into claptrap and deceit for fear of these million men armed with combustible fact. It would mean such an elevation of political discussion and political performance as democracy has never yet produced; such an elevation as democracy must produce or die.

Sex, Art, and Play in Social Reconstruction

So far our imagined Society has done no more than to seek and give information. It has, it is true, listened to propagandists and Utopians, and has published extracts from their testimony; but even this has been not to agitate but to inform; that such and such opinions are held by such and such men, and by such and such a number of men, is also a point of information. Merely to state facts is the essential thing, and the extremely effective thing. But now there are certain functions which such a Society might perform beyond the giving of facts - functions that involve personal attitudes and interpretations. It may be possible for our Society to take on these functions without detracting from the trust reposed in its statements of fact. What are these functions?

First of all, the stimulation of artistic production, and the extension of artistic appreciation. Our Society, which is composed of rather staid men, themselves not peculiarly fitted to pass judgment outside the field of science, will invite, let us say, twenty of the most generally and highly valued of English and American authors to form themselves into a Committee on Literary Awards, as a branch of the Society for Social Research. Imagine Thomas Hardy and George Bernard Shaw and H. G. Wells and John Galsworthy and Rudyard Kipling and John Masefield and George Moore and Joseph Conrad and W. D. Howells and Theodore Dreiser and many more, telling the world every month, in individual installments, their judgment on current fiction, drama, poetry, English literature in general; imagine the varied judgments printed with synoptic coordination of the results

322. Perhaps this million could be reached more surely and economically through direct pamphlet-publication by the Society.

as a way of fixing the standing of a book in the English literary world; and judge of the stimulus that would reside in lists signed by such names. Imagine another group of men, the literary elite of France, making briefer reports on French literature; and other groups in Germany, Russia, Italy, Spain, Scandinavia; imagine the world getting every month the judgment of Anatole France and Romain Rolland and Gerhardt Hauptmann and Anton Chekov and Georg Brandes on the current literature of their peoples; imagine them making lists, too, of the best books in all their literatures; imagine eager young men and women poring over these conflicting lists, discussing them, making lists of their own, and getting guidance so. And to the literary lists add monthly reports, by a committee of the Society itself, on the best books in the various fields of science. Finally, let the artists speak - painters and sculptors and all; let them say where excellence has dwelt this month in their respective fields. There are hundreds of thousands who hunger for such guidance as this plan would give. There are young people who flounder about hopelessly because they find no guidance; young people who are easily turned to fine work by the stimulus of responsible judgment, and as easily lapse into the banalities of popular fiction and popular magazines when this guiding stimulus fails to come. There are thousands of people who would be glad to pay their modest contribution to the support of any organization that would manage to get such direction for them. Half the value of a university course lies in this, that the teacher will suggest readings, judge books, and provide general guidance for individual work. Perhaps the most valuable kind of information in the world is that which guides one in the search for information. Such guidance, given to all who ask for it, would go far to save us from the mediocrity that almost stifles our national life.[323]

And more; why should not the stimulation be for the producers as well as for the consumers? Why should not some kind of award be made, say every six months, to the authors adjudged best in their lines by their qualified contemporaries? Why should such a book as *Jean Christophe* or *The Brothers Karamazov* go unheralded except in fragmentary individual ways? Why not reward such productions with a substantial prize? Or, if that be impossible, by some presentation of certificate? Even a "scrap of paper" would go a long way to stimulate the writer and guide the reader. But why should not a money reward be possible? If rich men will pay thousands upon thousands for the (perhaps) original works of dead artists, why should they not turn their wealth into spiritual gold by helping

---

323. Some students - e.g., Joseph McCabe, *The Tyranny of Shame*, London, 1916, p. 248 - are so impressed with the dangers lying in our vast production of written trash that they favor restricting the circulation of cheap fiction in our public libraries. But what we have to do is not to prohibit the evil but to encourage the good, to give positive stimulus rather than negative prohibition. People hate compulsion, but they grope for guidance.

the often impecunious writers of the living day? It is a convenient error to believe that financial aid would detract from the independence of the creator: it would, did it come from men rewarding on the basis of their own judgment; it would not if the judgment of the world's men of letters should be taken as criterion. And perhaps fewer Chattertons and Davidsons would mar the history of literature and art.

This direction of attention to what is best and greatest in the work of our age is a matter of deeper moment than superficial thought can grasp. If, by some such method, the meaning of "success" could be freed from monetary implication and attached rather to excellence in art and science, the change would have almost inestimably far-reaching results. Men worship money, as has often been pointed out, not for its own sake, nor for the material good it brings, but for the prestige of success that goes with its "conspicuous consumption"; let the artist find more appreciation for his ability than the captain of industry finds for his, and there will be a great release of energy from economic exploitation to creative work in science, literature, and art. A large part of the stimuli that prompt men to exploit their fellows will be gone; and that richest of all incentives - social esteem - will go to produce men eager to contribute to the general power and happiness of the community.[324]

The art impulse, as is generally believed, is a diversion of sex energy. An organism is essentially not a food-getting but a reproductive mechanism; the food-getting is a contributory incident in the reproduction. As development proceeds the period of pregnancy and adolescence increases, more of the offspring survive to maturity, large broods, litters, or families become unnecessary and more and more of the energy that was sexual slides over into originally secondary pursuits, like play and art. At the same time there is a gradual diminution in pugnacity (which was another factor in the drama of reproduction), and rivalry in games and arts encroaches more and more on the emotional field once monopolized by strife for mates and food. The game - a sort of Hegelian synthesis of hostility and sociability - takes more and more the place of war, and artistic creation increasingly replaces reproduction.

If all this is anything more than theoretic skating over thin sheets of fact, it means that one "way out" from our social perplexities lies in the provision of stronger stimulus to creation and recreation, art and games. It is a serious part of the social planner's work to find some way of nourishing the art impulse wherever it appears, and drawing it on by arranging rewards for its productions. And again we shall have to understand that play is an important matter in a nation's life; that one of the best signs for the future of America is the prevalence of healthy athleticism; and that

324. Cf. Russell, *Principles of Social Reconstruction.* p, 236: "The supreme principle, both in politics and in private life, should be to promote all that is creative, and so to diminish the impulses and desires that center round possession."

an attempt to widen these sport activities to greater intersectional and international scope than they have yet attained will get at some of the roots of international pugnacity. A wise government would be almost as interested in the people's games as in their schools, and would spend millions in making rivalry absorb the dangerous energy of pugnacity. Olympic games should not be Olympic games, occurring only with Olympiads; not a month should pass but great athletes, selected by eliminative tests from every part of every country, should meet, now here, now there, to match brawn and wits in the friendly enmity of games. Let men know one another through games, and they will not for slight reasons pass from sportsmanship to that competitive destruction and deceit which our political Barnums call "the defense of our national honor."

Education

This diversion of the sexual instinct into art and games (a prophylactic which has long since been applied to individuals, and awaits application to groups) must begin in the early days of personal development, so that our Society for Social Research would, if it were to take on this task, find itself inextricably mixed up with the vast problem of educational method and aim.

Here more than anywhere one hears the call for enlightenment and sees the need for clarification. Here is an abundance of *'isms* and a dearth of knowledge. Most teachers use methods which they themselves consider antiquated, and teach subjects which they will admit not one in a hundred of their pupils will ever need to know. Curious lessons in ethics are administered, which are seldom practiced in the classroom, and make initiative children come to believe that commandment-breaking is heroic. Boys and girls bursting with vitality and the splendid exuberance of youth are cramped for hours into set positions, while by a sort of water-cure process knowledge is pumped into them from books duller than a doctor's dissertation in philosophy.

And so forth: the indictment against our schools has been drawn up a thousand times and in a thousand ways, and needs no reinforcement here. But though we have indicted we have not made any systematic attempt to find just what is wrong, and how, and where; and what may be done to remedy the evil. Experiments have been made, but their bearings and results have been very imperfectly recorded.

Suppose now that our Society for Social Research should appoint a great Committee on Education to hire expert investigators and make a thorough attempt to clarify the issues in education. Here the function of philosophy should be clear; for the educator touches at almost every point those problems of values, individual and social, which are the special hunting ground of the philosopher. The importance of psychology here is recognized, but the importance of biology and pathology has not been seen in fit perspective. Why should not a special group of men be set aside for years, if necessary, to study the applicability of the several sciences to education? Why should not all scientific knowledge, so far as it touches human nature, be focused on the semi-darkness in which the educator works?

Two special problems in this field invite research. One concerns the effect, on national character and capacity, of a system of education controlled by the government. The point was made by Spinoza, as may be remembered, that a government will, if it controls the schools, aim to restrain rather than to develop the energies of men. Kant remarked the same difficulty. The function of education in the eyes of a dominant class is to make men able to do skilled work but unable to do original thinking (for all original thinking begins with destruction); the function of education in the eyes of a government is to teach men that eleventh commandment which God forgot to give to Moses: thou shalt love thy country right or wrong. All this, of course, requires some marvelous prestidigitation of the truth, as school textbooks of national history show. The ignorant, it seems, are the necessary ballast in the ship of state.

The alternative to such schools seems to be a return to private education, with the rich man's son getting even more of a start on the poor boy than he gets now. Is there a *tertium quid* here? Perhaps this is one point which a resolute effort to get the facts would clarify. What does such governmentally-regulated education do to the forces of personal difference and initiative? Will men and women educated in such a way produce their maximum in art and thought and industry? Or will they be automata, always waiting for a push? What different results would come if the nationally-owned schools were to confine their work absolutely to statements of fact, presentations of science, and were to leave "character-molding" and lessons in ethics to private persons or institutions? Then at least each parent might corrupt his own child in his own pet way; and there might be a greater number of children who would not be corrupted at all.

Another problem which might be advanced towards a solution by a little light is that of giving higher education to those who want it but are too poor to pay. There are certain studies, called above the social disciplines, which help a man not so much to raise himself out of his class and become a snob, as to get a better understanding of himself and his fellow-men. Since mutual understanding is a hardly exaggerable social good, why should not a way be found to provide for all who wish it evening instruction in history, sociology, economics, psychology, biology, philosophy, and similar fields of knowledge? Every added citizen who has received instruction in these matters is a new asset to the community; he will vote with more intelligence, he will work better in cooperation, he will be less subject to undulations of social mania, he will be a hint to all office-seekers to put their usual nonsense on the shelf. Perhaps by this medium too our Society would spread its reports and widen its influence. Imagine a nation of people instructed in these sciences: with such a people civilization would begin.

And then again, our busy-body Society would turn its research light on the universities, and tell them a thing or two of what the light would show. It would betray the lack of coordination among the various sciences - the department of psychology, for example, never coming to so much as speaking terms with the department of economics; it would call for an extension, perhaps, of the now infrequent seminars and conferences between departments whose edges overlap, or which shed light on a common field. It would invite the university to give less of its time to raking over the past, and help it to orient itself toward the future; it would suggest to every university that it provide an open forum for the responsible expression of all shades of opinion; it would, in general, call for a better organization of science as part of the organization of intelligence; it would remind the universities that they are more vital even than governments; and it might perhaps succeed in getting engraved on the gates of every institution of learning the words of Thomas Hobbes: "Seeing the universities are the foundation of civil and moral doctrine, from whence the preachers and the gentry, drawing such water as they find, use to sprinkle the same upon the people, there ought certainly to be great care taken to have it pure."

CHAPTER NINE
THE READER SPEAKS

The Democratization of Aristocracy

And now we stop for objections.

"This plan is a hare-brained scheme for a new priesthood and a new aristocracy. It would put a group of college professors and graduates into a position where they could do almost as they please. You think you avoid this by telling the gentlemen that they must limit themselves to the statement of fact; but if you knew the arts of journalism you would not make so naive a distinction between airing opinions and stating facts. When a man buys up a newspaper what he wants to do is not so much to control the editorials as to 'edit' the news - that is, to select the facts which shall get into print. It's wonderful what lies you can spread without telling lies. For example, if you want to hurt a public man, you quote all his foolish speeches and ignore his wise ones; you put his mistakes into headlines and hide his achievements in a corner.[325] I will guarantee to prove anything I like, or anything I don't like, just by stating facts. So with your Society for Social Research; it would become a great political, rather than an educational, organization; it would almost unconsciously select its information to suit its hobbies. Why, the thing is psychologically impossible. If you want something to be true you will be half blind and half deaf to anything that obstructs your desire; that is the way we're made. And even if nature did not attend to this, money would: as soon as your society exercised real power on public opinion it would be bought up, in a gentle, sleight-of-hand way, by some economic group; a few of the more influential members of the Society would be 'approached,' some 'present' would be made, and justice would have another force to contend with. No; your Society won't do!"

Well, let us see. Here you have a body of 5000 men; rather a goodly number for even an American millionaire to purchase. They wish to investigate, say, the problem of birth control; what do they do? They vote, without nominations, for six of their number to manage the investigation; the six men receiving the highest vote investigate and write out a report. Now

---

325. This passage undoubtedly brings to mind the press' treatment of the United States' current president, George Bush, whose verbal slips are always seized upon by the press.

if any report were published which misstated facts, or omitted important items, the fault would at once diminish the repute and influence of the Society. Let merely the suspicion get about that these reports are unfair, and the Society would begin to decay. That is, the power of the Society would grow with its fairness and fall with its unfairness - a very happy arrangement. The fear of this fall in influence would be the best incentive to impartial reports. Every committee would feel that the future of the Society depended on the fairness of its own report; and every man on every committee would hesitate before making himself responsible for the disrepute of the Society; he would feel himself on trial before his fellow-members, and would halt himself in the natural slide into partiality.

Not that he would always succeed; men are men. But it is reasonable to expect that men working under these conditions would be considerably more impartial than the average newspaper. Again, who is as impartial as the scientist? One cannot do much in science without a stern control of the personal equation; to describe protozoa, for example, as one would like them to be, is no very clever way of attaining repute in protozoology. This is not so true in the social as in the physical sciences, though even in this new field scientific fairness and accuracy are rapidly increasing. One can get more reliable and impartial reports of an industrial situation - e.g., of the Colorado troubles - from the scientific investigators than from either side to the controversy. The very deficiencies of the student type - incapacity for decisions or for effective methods in action - involve a compensatory grasp of understanding and impartiality of attitude. Our best guarantee against dishonesty is not virtue but intelligence, and our Society is supposed to be a sort of distilled Intelligence.

That the scheme savors of aristocracy is not to its discredit. We need aristocracy, in the sense of better methods for giving weight to superior brains; we need a touch of Plato in our democracy. After all, the essence of the plan, as we have said, is the democratization of Plato and Nietzsche and Carlyle; the intelligent man gets more political power, but only through the mechanism of democracy. His greater power comes not by his greater freedom to do what he pleases despite the majority, but by improved facilities for enlightening and converting the majority. Democracy, ideally, means only that the aristocracy is periodically elected and renewed; and this is a plan whereby the aristocrats - the really best - shall be more clearly seen to be so. Furthermore, the plan avoids the great defect of Plato's scheme - that philosophers are not fitted for executive and administrative work, that those skilled to see are very seldom also able to do. Here the philosopher, the man who gets at the truth, rules, but only indirectly, and without the burdens of office and execution. And indeed it is not the philosopher who rules, but truth. The liberator is made king.

The Professor as Buridan's Ass[326]

"You have anticipated my objection, and cleverly twisted it into an argument. But that would be too facile an escape; you must face more squarely the fact that your professors are mere intellectualist highbrows, incapable of understanding the real issues involved in our social war, and even more incapable of suggesting practical ways out. The more you look the more you see; the more you see, the less you do. You think that reflection leaves you peace of mind; it doesn't, it leaves your mind in pieces. The intellectual is like Dr. Buridan's ass: he is so careful to stand in the middle that he never gives a word of practical advice, for fear that he will compromise himself and fracture a syllogism. The trouble is that we think too much, not too little; we make thinking a substitute for action. Really, as Rousseau argued, thinking is unnatural; what the world needs is men who can make up their minds and then march on, almost in blinders, to a goal. We know enough, we know too much; and surely we have a plethora of investigating committees. A committee is just a scientific way of doing nothing. Your plan would flood the country with committees and leave courage buried under facts. You should call your organization a Society for Talky-talk."

The only flaw in this argument is that it does not touch the proposal. What is suggested is not that the Society take action or make programs, much less execute them; we ask our professors merely to do for a larger public, and more thoroughly and systematically, what we are glad to have them do for a small number of us in college and university. Action is *ex hypothesi* left to others; the function of the researcher is quite simply to look and tell us what he sees. That he is a highbrow, an intellectual, and even a Buridan's ass, does not interfere with his seeing; nobody ever argued that Buridan's ass was blind.

We forget that seeing is itself an art. Some of us have specialized in the art, and have naturally failed to develop cleverness in practical affairs. But that does not mean that our special talent cannot be used by the community, any more than Sir Oliver Lodge's fondness for celestial exploration makes us reject his work on electricity. Thinking is itself a form of action, and not the easiest nor the least effective. It is true that "if you reflect too much you will never accomplish anything," but if you reflect too little you will accomplish about as much. We make headway only by the head way. Action without forethought tends to follow a straight line; but in life the straight line is often the longest distance between two points,

326. "Buridan's Ass" refers to refers to a paradoxical anecdote related by French philosopher Jean Buridan in which "an ass, standing equidistant between two identical bales of hay, is faced with the choice of feasting on one or the other. All things being equal, the ass starves to death because there's no rational reason for choosing one bale over the other." (Source: www.buridansass.com) The situation is used to demonstrate the impracticality of making choices according to a formal system of reasoning.

because, as Leonardo said, the straightest line offers the greatest resistance.

Thought is roundabout, and loves flank attacks. The man of action rushes into play courageously, succeeds now, fails then; and sooner or later wishes - if he lives to wish - that he could think more. The increasing dependence of industry on scientific research, and of politics on expert investigators, shows how the world is coming to value the man whose specialty is seeing. Faith in intellect, as Santayana says, "is the only faith yet sanctioned by its fruit."[327] The two most important men in America just now are, or have been, college professors. To speak still more boldly: the greatest single human source of good in our generation is the "intellectual" researcher and professor. The man to be feared above all others is the man who can see.

Is Information Wanted?

"But your whole scheme shows a very amateur knowledge of human nature. You seem to think you can get people interested in fact. You can't; fact is too much against their interest. If the facts favor their wish, they are interested; if not, they forget them. The hardest thing in the world is to listen to truth that threatens to frustrate desire. That is why people won't listen to your reports, unless you tell them what they want to hear. They will - and perhaps excusably - prefer the bioscope to your embalmed statistics; just as they will prefer to read *The Family Herald* rather than the subtleties recommended by the Mutual Admiration Society which you would make out of our men of letters. You can investigate till you are blue in the face, and all you will get out of it won't be worth the postage stamps you use. Public opinion doesn't follow fact, it follows desire; people don't vote for a man because he is supported by 'truth' but because he promises to do something they like. And the man who makes the biggest promises to the biggest men will get office 99 times out of 100, no matter what the facts are. What counts is not truth but money."

This is the basic difficulty. Is it worth while to spread information? Think how much information is spread every week in Europe and America - the world remaining the while as "wicked" as it probably ever was. Public opinion is still, it seems, as Sir Robert Peel described it to be: "a compound of folly, weakness, prejudice, wrong feeling, right feeling, obstinacy, and newspaper paragraphs,"[328] - particularly the paragraphs. Once we thought that the printing press was the beginning of democracy, that Gutenberg had enfranchised the world. Now it appears that print and plutocracy get along very well together. Nevertheless, the hope of the weak

---

327. *Reason in Common Sense*, New York, 1911, p. 96.
328. Quoted by Walter Weyl, *The New Democracy*, p. 136.

lies in numbers and in information - in democracy and in print. "The remedy for the abuses of public opinion is not to discredit it but to instruct it."[329] The cure for misstatements is better statements. If the newspapers are used to spread falsehood, that is no reason why newspapers should not be used to spread truth. After all, the spread of information has done many things: killed dogma, sterilized many marriages, and even prevented wars; and there is no reason why a further spread may not do more valuable things than any yet done. It has been said, so often that we are apt to admit it just to avoid its repetition, that discussion affects nothing. But indeed nothing else affects anything. Whatever is done without information and discussion is soon undone, must be soon undone; all that bears time is that which survives the test of thought. All problems are at last problems in information: to find out just how things stand is the only finally effective way of getting at anything.

As to the limited number of persons who would be reached by the reports, let us not ask too much. There is no pretense here that the great mass of the people would be reached; no doubt these would go on living what Wells calls the "normal social life." But these people do not count for constructive purposes; they divide about evenly in every election. The men who do count - the local leaders, the clergymen, the lecturers, the teachers, the union officials, the newspaper men, the "agitators," the arch-rebels and the arch-Tories - all these men will be reached; and the information given will strengthen some and weaken others, and so play its effective part in the drama of social change. Each one of these men will be a center for the further distribution of information. Imagine a new monthly with a country-wide circulation of one million voters (that is, a general circulation of five million); would such a periodical have power? Would not millions be given to control it? Well, here we have more power, because not so concentrated in a few editorial hands, not so easily purchasable, and based on better intellect and repute. The money that would be paid at any time for the control of a periodical of such influence would finance our Society for many years.

It is impossible to believe that such a spread of knowledge as is here suggested would do nothing to elevate the moral and political life of the country. Consider the increased scrupulousness with which a Congressman would vote if he knew that at the next election his record would be published in cold print in a hundred newspapers, over the name of the Society for Social Research. Consider the effect, on Congressional appropriations for public buildings, of a plain statement of the population and size of the towns which require such colossal edifices for their mail. Publicity, it has been said, is the only cure for bad motives. Consider the stimulus which such reports would give to political discussion every-

---

329. Ross, *Social Control*, New York. 1906, p. 103.

where. Hardly a dispute occurs which is not based upon insufficient acquaintance with the facts; here would be information up to date, ready to give the light which dispels the heat. Men would turn to these reports all the more willingly because the reports were pledged to confine themselves to fact. Men would find here no attacks, no argument, no theory or creed; it would be refreshing, in some ways, to bathe the mind, hot with contention, in these cool streams of fact, and to emerge cleansed of error and filled with the vitality of truth. We have spent so much time attacking what we hate that we have not stopped to tell people what we like; if we would only affirm more and deny less there would be less of cross-purpose in the world. And information is affirmation. It would not open the wounds of controversy so much as offer points of contact; and in the light of fact, enemies might see that their good lay for the most part on a common road. If you want to change a foe into a friend (or, some cynic will say, a friend into a foe), give him information.

Finding Maecenas[330]

"Well; suppose you are right. Suppose information, as you say, is king. How are you going to do it? Do you really think you will get some benevolent millionaire to finance you? And will you, like Fourier, wait in your room every day at noon for the man who will turn your dream into a fact?"

What we tend to forget about rich men is that besides being rich they are men. There are a surprising number of them - particularly those who have inherited money - who are eager to return to the community - the larger part of their wealth, if only they could be shown a way of doing it which would mean more than a change of pockets. Merely to give to charity is, in Aristotle's phrase, to pour water into a leaking cask. What such men want is a way of increasing intelligence; they know from hard experience that in the end intelligence is the quality to be desired and produced. They have spent millions, perhaps billions, on education; and this plan of ours is a plan for education. If it is what it purports to be, some one of these men will offer to finance it.

And not only one. Let the beginnings of our Society be sober and efficient, let its first investigations be thorough and intelligent, let its initial reports be impartial, succinct, illuminating and simple, and further help will come almost unasked. After a year of honest and capable work our Society would find itself supported by rather a group of men than by one man; it might conceivably find itself helped by the state, at the behest of the citizens. What would prevent a candidate for governor from declaring

---

330. Gaius Maecenas was a political advisor of Caesar Augustus and a particularly charitable patron of the arts; his name has become synonymous with the idea of the wealthy benefactor.

his intention that should he be elected he would secure an annual appropriation for our Society? And why should not the voters be attracted by such a declaration? Why should not the voters demand such a declaration?

Nor need we fear that a Society so helped by the rich man and the state would turn into but one more instrumentality of obstructionism. Not that such an organization of intelligence would be "radical": the words "radical" and "conservative" have become but instruments of calumny, and truth slips between them. But in the basic sense of the word our Society would be extremely radical; for there is nothing so radical, so revolutionary, as just to tell the truth, to say what it is you see. That surely is to go to the *radix* of the thing. And truth has this advantage: that it is discriminately revolutionary: there are some things old to which truth is no enemy, just as there are some things new which will melt in the glare of fact. Let the fact say.

This is the final faith: that truth will make us free, so far as we can ever be free. Let the truth be published to the world, and men separated in the dark will see one another, and one another's purposes, more clearly, and with saner understanding than before. The most disastrous thing you can do to an evil is to describe it. Let truth be told, and the parasite will lose his strength through shame, and meanness will hide its face. Only let information be given to all and freely, and it will be a cleansing of our national blood; enmity will yield to open and honest opposition, where it will not indeed become cooperation. All we need is to see better. Let there be light.

The Chance of Philosophy

"One more objection before you take the money. And that is: What on earth has all this to do with philosophy? I can understand that to have economists on your investigating committees, and biologists, and psychologists, and historians, would be sensible; but what could a philosopher do? These are matters for social science, not for metaphysics. Leave the philosophers out and some of us may take your scheme seriously."

It is a good objection, if only because it shows again the necessity for a new kind of philosopher. Merely to make such an objection is to reinforce the indictment brought above against the philosopher as he is. But what of the philosopher as he might be?

What might the philosopher be?

Well, first of all, he would be a living man, and not an annotator of the past. He would have grown freely, his initial spark of divine fire unquenched by scholastic inflexibilities of discipline and study. He would have imbibed no sermons, but his splendid curiosity would have found food and encouragement from his teachers. He would have lived in and learned to love the country and the city; he would be at home in the ploughed fields as well as in the centers of learning; he would like the cleansing solitude of the woods and yet too the invigorating bustle of the city streets. He would be brought up on Plato and Thucydides, Leonardo and Michelangelo, Bacon and Montaigne; he would study the civilization of Greece and that of the Renaissance on all sides, joining the history of politics, economics, and institutions with that of science, literature, and philosophy; and yet he would find time to study his own age thoroughly. He would be interested in life, and full of it; he would jump into campaigns, add his influence carefully to movements he thought good, and help make the times live up more nearly to their possibilities. He would not shut himself up forever in laboratories, libraries, and lecture rooms; he would live more widely than that. He would be of the earth earthly, of the world worldly. He would not talk of ideals in the abstract and do nothing for them in the concrete; above all else in the world he would abhor the kind of talk that is a refuge from the venture and responsibility of action. He would not only love wisdom, he would live it.

But we must not make our ideal philosopher too repulsively perfect. Let us agree at least to this, that a man who should know the social disciplines, and not merely one science, would be of help in some such business as we have been proposing; and if we suppose that he has not only knowledge but wisdom, that his acquaintance with the facts of science is matched by his knowledge of life, that through fellowship with genius in Greece and Florence he has acquired a fund of wisdom which needs but the nourishment of living to grow richer from day to day, then we are on the way to seeing that this is the sort of man our Society would need above all other sorts of men. Such philosophers would be worthy to guide research and direct the enlightenment of the world; such philosophers might be to their generation what Socrates and Plato were to their generations and Francis Bacon to his; such a philosophy, in Nietzsche's words, might rule!

This is the chance of philosophy. It may linger further in that calm death of social ineffectiveness in which we see it sinking; or it may catch the hands of the few philosophers who insist on focusing thought on life, and so regain the position which it alone is fitted to fill. Unless that position is filled, and properly, all the life of the world is zigzag and fruitless - what we have called the logic-chopping life; and unless that position is filled philosophy too is logic-chopping, zigzag, and fruitless, and turns away from life men whom life most sorely needs. There are some among us, even some philosophers among us, who are eager to lead the way out of bickering into discussion, out of criticism into construction, out of books into life. We must keep a keen eye for such men - and their beginnings - and we must strengthen them with our little help. Philosophy is too divinely splendid a thing to be kept from the most divine of things - creation. Some of us love it as the very breath of our lives; it is our vital medium, without which life would be less than vegetation, and we will not rest so long as the name *philosopher* means anything less aspiring and inspiring than it did with Plato. Science flourishes and philosophy languishes, because science is honest and philosophy sycophantic, because science touches life and helps it, while philosophy shrinks fearfully and helplessly away. If philosophy is to live again, it must rediscover life, it must come back into the cave, it must come down from the "real" and transcendental world and play its venturesome part in the hard and happy world of efforts and events.

It is the chance of philosophy.

CONCLUSION

See now, in summary, how modest a suggestion it is, grandiloquent though it may have seemed. We propose no 'ism, we make no program; we suggest, tentatively, a method. We propose a new start, a new tack, a new approach - not to the exclusion of other approaches, but to their assistance. If this thing should be done, it would not mean that other gropers toward a better world would have to stand idle; it would but give light to them that walk in darkness. And it would make possible a more generous cooperation among the different currents in the stream of reconstructive thought.

We are a little discouraged today; we lovers of the new have become doubtful of the object of our love. Perhaps - we sometimes feel - all this effort is a vain circling in the mist; perhaps we do not advance, but only move. Our faith in progress is dimmed. We even tire of the "social problem"; we have tried so many ways, knocked at so many doors, and found so little of that which we sought. Sometimes, in the lassitude of mistaken effort and drear defeat, we almost think that the social problem is never to find even partial solution, that it is not a problem but a limitation, a limitation forever. We need a new beginning, a new impetus - perhaps a new delusion?

See, too, how the thought of our five teachers lies concentrated and connected in this new approach: what have we done but renew concretely the Socratic plea for intelligence, the Platonic hope for philosopher-kings, Bacon's dream of knowledge organized and ruling the world, Spinoza's gentle insistence on democracy as the avenue of development, and Nietzsche's passionate defense of aristocracy and power? There was something in us that thrilled at Plato's conception of a philosophy that could guide as well as dissect our social life; but there was another something in us that hesitated before his plan of slavery as the basis of it all. We felt that we would rather be free and miserable than bound and filled. Why should a man feed himself if his feet are chained, and he must never move? And we were inspired, too, by the demand that the best should rule, that they should have power fitted to their worth; we should be glad to find some way whereby the best could have power, could rule, and yet with the consent of all - we wanted an aristocracy sanctioned by democracy, a social order standing on the broad base of free citizenship and wide cooperation. Socrates shows us how to use Bacon to reconcile Plato and Nietzsche with Spinoza: intelligence will organize intelligence so that superior worth may have superior influence and yet work with and through the will of all.

And here at the end comes a thought that some of us perhaps have had more than once as this discussion advanced: *What could the Church do for the organization of intelligence?*

It could do wonderful things. It has power, organization, facilities, through which the gospel of "the moral obligation to be intelligent" could be preached to a wider audience than any newspaper could reach. And among the clergy are hundreds of young men who have found new inspiration in the figure of Jesus seen through the aspirations of democracy; hundreds eager to do their part in any work that will lessen the misery of men. What if they were to find in this organization of intelligence a focus for their labor? What if they should not only themselves undertake the studies which would fit them for membership in the Society, but should also make it their business to stir up in all who might come to them the spirit of the seeker, to incite them to read religiously the reports of the Society, to call on them to spread abroad the good news of truth to be had for the asking? What if these men should make their churches extension centers for the educational work of the Society - giving freely the use of their halls and even contributing to the expense of organizing classes and paying for skilled instruction? What if they should see in the spread of intelligence the best avenue to that wide friendship which Jesus so passionately preached? What better way is there to make men love one another than to make men understand one another? True charity comes only with clarity, just as "mercy" is but justice that understands. Surely the root of all evil is the inability to see clearly that which is; how better can religion combat evil than to preach clarity as the beginning of social redemption?

One of the many burdens that drag on the soul is a knowledge of the past. It is a strong man who can know history and keep his courage; a great dream that can face the fact and live. We look at those flitting experiments called civilizations: we see them rise one after another, we see them produce and produce and produce, we feel the weight of their accumulating wealth; still visionable to us the busyness of geniuses and slaves piling stone upon stone and making pyramids to greet the stars, still audible the voices of Socrates in the agora and of old Plato passing quietly among the students in the grove, still haunting us the white faces of martyrs in the amphitheatres of Rome: and then the pyramids stand bare and lonely, the voices of Greek genius are hushed, the Coliseum is a ruin and a memory; one after another these peoples pass, these wonderful peoples, greater perhaps, wiser and nobler perhaps, than the peoples of our time; and we almost choke with the heavy sense of a vast futility encompassing the world. Some of us turn away then from the din of effort, and seek in resignation the comfort of a living death; some others find in the doubt and difficulty the zest and reward of the work. After all, the past is not dead, it has not failed; only the vileness of it is dead, gone with the winnowing of time; that which was great and worthy lives and works and is real. Plato speaks to us still, speaks to millions and millions of us, and the blood of martyrs is the seed of saints. We speak and pass, but the word remains. Effort is not lost, *not to have tried* is the only failure, the only misery; all effort is happiness, all effort is success. And so again we write ourselves in books and stone and color, and smile in the face of time; again we hear the call of the work, that it be done:

> *Edens that wait the wizardry of thought,*
> *Beauty that craves the touch of artist hands,*
> *Truth that but hungers to be felt or seen;*

and again we are hot with the passion for perfection. We will remake. We will wonder and desire and dream and plan and try. We are such beings as dream and plan and try; and the glory of our defeats dims the splendor of the sun. We will take thought and add a cubit to our stature; we will bring intelligence to the test and call it together from all corners of the earth; we will harness the genius of the race and renew creation.

We will remake.

www.ingramcontent.com/pod-product-compliance
Lightning Source LLC
Chambersburg PA
CBHW071132280326
41935CB00010B/1201